BLESSINGS

for

LOVE & WAR

by
Jan Elkins

with
Anna Elkins

Listening Heart
PO Box 509
Jacksonville, OR 97530 USA
jan@livingwatersmedford.org
ISBN-13: 978-0692777411
ISBN-10: 0692777415

Cover design by Anna Elkins

Printed in the United States of America

DEDICATION

I dedicate this book of blessings to our children, Anna and David. God's words awaken you to life and love. These blessings are your inheritance.

Also by Jan Elkins:

A Book of Blessings

CONTENTS

FOREWORD

A few years ago, I took a screenwriting workshop for fun. The thing I most remember was a producer's comment that all great stories throughout human existence center on some aspect of love or war.

When my mother, Jan, told me she was working on another book of blessings, I asked her if this one had a theme. She told me she had been writing blessings inspired by Song of Songs and blessings on spiritual warfare from her life experience.

Love and war. The title came just like that: *Blessings for Love and War*.

Paul's letters to the Corinthians contain the keys for both:

Love is patient, love is kind. It does not envy, it does not boast, it is not proud. It does not dishonor others, it is not self-seeking, it is not easily angered, it keeps no record of wrongs. Love does not delight in evil but rejoices with the truth. It always protects, always trusts, always hopes, always perseveres.

—I Corinthians 13: 4-7 NIV

For though we live in the world, we do not wage war as the world does.

—II Corinthians 10:3 NIV

We all engage in everyday stories of love and war—small scale and large. And, whether we acknowledge it or not, we also engage in those stories in the supernatural—in realms we can't always see but which are more real than the ones we can.

These blessings are tools for loving well and fighting well. Wield them with love and honor.

—Anna Elkins

5

INTRODUCTION

These blessings are written from the Scriptures. Many are inspired by Old Covenant Scriptures with a New Covenant understanding of Jesus, the Cross, and Resurrection.

Blessings have not been taught much in modern times, even though the Bible is full of them. Jesus made declarations in the Sermon on the Mount that we are blessed (fully satisfied) in Him. Paul repeatedly blesses the churches in his letters.

A blessing can be spoken as a word of encouragement, a declaration, a promise, a proclamation, or as a prophetic word.

A blessing is an impartation of the Living Word, Himself. When I bless someone, I am taking the living Word of God from the pages of Scripture and "breathing" those words (speaking them) into a person's life. God's words are alive and powerful. When spoken, they shift the spiritual environment.

How I Learned the Power of the Living Word

In 1981, I had a heart-to-heart conversation with God about a problem. I had married a policeman who was now entering a new, life-changing assignment: he was going to be a pastor. I struggled with yielding to this change in plans.

The very reason I had waited so long to follow Jesus wholeheartedly in my life was the fear that He would ask me to go someplace I did not want to go or to do something I thought I could not do. The thought of pastoring a church triggered all of those fears.

Eventually, I asked Jesus to give me His desire and a calling to pastor, as well. Otherwise, I knew it would not work.

It was now coming up on the fourth year since that prayer. Pioneering a new church was way beyond me in every way. There we were, caring for a new family of almost two hundred people we loved. Yet, I felt so poorly equipped, especially in the Scriptures. I had a scattered, selective interest in God's Word. I was an avid reader in general, but not for the Bible.

Up until 1979, my understanding of a speaking God had been almost exclusively through the written Word. The "Trinity" had looked more like God the Father, Jesus the Son, and the Holy Bible. But if God had only spoken to create the Bible, how could I respond to it as a living book?

I had another heart-to-heart talk with God. I told Him I felt like a failure. My days were a series of interruptions and to-do lists. I struggled to be consistent and inspired. Without pastoral teachings or authors like Oswald Chambers, the deficit would have been much worse. So I asked God for *His* desire for me. I asked Him to help me love Him so much I would love His Word.

Not long after, I read an obscure verse in Job about treasuring the words of His mouth even more than food (23:12). Job was talking about a personal God whose words he treasured.

A thought came to me: I wanted to treasure God's Word even more than food. Following the Voice, I committed to spending a minimum of 15 minutes with Jesus each day before I ate breakfast. I thought that maybe a brief time was better than nothing and would build consistency.

The following day, our family started early as usual. We always ate breakfast and dinner together as a family, even through the kids' years in high school. I cooked and served and we sat together. I didn't draw attention to the fact that I wasn't eating.

When Garris drove the kids to school, I sat down for my time to read the Word. Over the following couple of weeks, something shifted. I began to hear God's voice more consistently and clearly. I had increasing stretches of time with Jesus. My heart was awakening to Him in a fresh way. Soon I no longer needed to go without breakfast.

I learned that God wasn't counting against me the times I missed having my "devotions." He was joyful to commune with me every time I desired Him above my schedule and to-do list. He loved to talk with me and spend time with me. He longed for me to pursue Him. He wanted to carry the burdens I dutifully tended and regularly tried to pick back up.

My husband often says, "All breakthrough begins

with a word from God." It was in those morning times with God that I received both a calling to pastor and a love for His Word.

I now love to bless others with His Word—His living word of truth and love and freedom, empowered through an impartation of the Holy Spirit.

Yes indeed, it won't be long now. God's Decree. Things are going to happen so fast your head will swim, one thing fast on the heels of the other. You won't be able to keep up. Everything will be happening at once—and everywhere you look, blessings! Blessings like wine pouring off the mountains and hills.

—Amos 9:13, *The Message*

Blessing of Belief
Hebrews 1:1-2

In the name of Jesus Christ,
    I bless your spirit with belief.
The language of God is through His Son—
    Jesus is the language of God.

Jesus created the complete span of all existence:
    He formed the earth in the beginning,
    He crafted the cosmos—
    the panorama of all universes
    and all time.

Jesus is the mirror image of God—
    the image of His glory,
    the exact expression of His true nature,
    the reflection and shining
    radiance of His splendor.

Jesus is Almighty!
By the power of His spoken word,
    He holds the universe together
    and expands it.

I bless your spirit with belief in His words
    spoken to you through all
    methods of communication—
    at any price,
    in every way, shape and form—
    in the name of Jesus Christ.

His written Word is the outcome of His voice—
    His thoughts,
    His will, His character,
    His goodness—
    put in words that you can hear.

Jesus is not limited to a book
    with ink on pages.
He is speaking in the universe He created—
    a universe that cannot contain Him.
He is speaking now,
    not just a long time ago.

Darkness heard Him and became light;
    He is speaking into your darkness
    and creating light.
Chaos heard Him and became order;
    He is speaking to your chaos
    and bringing order.

I bless you with belief
    that Jesus is speaking to you personally—
    that it is His nature to speak
    and that He has never stopped speaking.

He is holding you together,
    building one truth upon another,
    putting the pieces together—
    expanding the revelation of Himself
    by His spoken word to you.
His word will remain forever.

The enemy knows those
   who know the voice of God;
   he will run from those
   who are yielded to the Living Word.
I bless you with breakthrough
   that begins with a word from God.

BLESSINGS FOR LOVE

These blessings come in two parts: Part I contains general blessings for love and Part II contains blessings from Song of Songs.

PART I:
GENERAL BLESSINGS FOR LOVE

Blessing of the Best
John 2:1-11

For His first miracle, Jesus used six large clay jars with a combined capacity of 120-150 gallons of water. This water was used for the Jewish washing rituals as an outward purification for worshippers coming into a synagogue. Jesus turned the water in these vessels into the finest wine to be joyfully consumed. It was a prophetic picture and promise of Holy Spirit baptism.

I wrote this blessing from a prophecy I gave to a friend. For those of you who are waiting for a promise to be fulfilled, the waiting is worth it. God is known to save His best for last. Whether your promise—your "wine"—comes instantaneously and turns out to be the best, or whether it is the best because it has matured in the waiting, it is a good gift from a good God!

In the name of Jesus Christ,
    I bless your spirit with joyful
    anticipation of promises fulfilled.

In the waiting, a miracle unfolds.
At the wedding feast,
    Jesus changed jars of water
    into the very best wine—
    the most perfect wine of all the ages.

Jesus does not withhold joy;
    He loves to feast and celebrate with you.
The purifying water of the Word of God

becomes the wine of the Spirit,
bearing the fruit of joy.

He extends joy to you,
He takes delight in your joy—
there is no limit of joy available to you!
May your heart be undone
by the exquisite miracle reserved for you.

In the waiting—
even when you are running out of time,
even when worry sets in—
the waiting is worth it.

Whatever Jesus tells you to do,
make sure to do it:
His ways are perfect,
His timing is right.
In the waiting,
the majestic glory of Jesus
is evidenced by a miracle.

I bless you with fulfillment of promise—
the wonder of getting to proclaim these words:

Jesus, you saved the best until last!
You are the Promise.
In you, I dwell in promise.
I receive your promise.
My hope is a substance—
a reality—secure in you.

Blessing of a Fresh Start
Psalm 85

Our daughter, Anna, created a painting depicting a section of Psalm 85. I turned that Psalm into a blessing.

Be outrageously blessed,
    in the name of Jesus Christ.
The Lord has poured out so many blessings:
    He has led you out of captivity,
    He has covered every sin,
    He has restored your destiny.
Pause in His presence—
    bask in His glorious,
    undeniable, relentless love.

God's blazing anger at injustice has ended—
    extinguished by His mercy.
Jesus bore God's full judgment,
    satisfying every letter of the law—
    His ultimate sacrifice sufficient
    for all mankind:
    He forgives you,
    He lifts your guilt,
    He delivers you,
    He turns your sorrow to joy,
    He showers you with blessings.

Cry out to God:

    Revive me!

Restore me back to you.
Bring me back to loving you.

Abba, Father, pour out more of your love.
Reveal more of your heart—
more of your kindness,
more of your peace,
more of your glory.

You are blessed because you call out to God:
    He is close to you,
    He responds to your cry,
    He gives you resurrection life,
    He pronounces you whole and well,
    He gives you a fresh start.

Listen carefully for His voice.
Wait to hear what He will say—
    receive His promise of peace.

God's love for you is immeasurable—
    Oh, how He loves you!
In receiving His love,
    you will respond with love,
    you will taste joy and gladness.

I declare that you are home base for Glory!
You are a landing zone
    for the glory of God—you,
    your family, the generations after you,
    your home, your land.

You are blessed as Mercy and Truth meet
    face to face,
    embracing each other,
    empowering you to right living.

Righteousness pours down from Heaven
    and kisses peace—imparting whole living.
Goodness rains down in torrents!
His Presence shines on you.

Beauty touches you, awakening you to life.
Truth springs up—
    flourishing in vibrant hues of color.
Faithfulness is in full bloom.

I bless you with great abundance—
    blessings upon blessings upon blessings.
Be drenched with bounty and blessing.

Jesus is your way-maker of deliverance and peace.
He strides out in front of you,
    clearing a pathway.
Be blessed as you follow in His footsteps.

Blessing of Love's Essence
I John 4:18; II Timothy 1:7

Sometimes it is hard to identify what is troubling me. I can tell what the real problem is by asking myself questions: "What is my fear?" And," What do I need/want?"

For example, I need love. I was created for love. My goal in life is to live encompassed in God's love. Fear is an indicator that I'm not receiving what He has already given to me. Identify your fear; it will lead you to a need. Do you need love? Make an exchange by lifting the requirement that another person or a circumstance fulfill that need. Turn to Jesus and receive from Him what you need. He is Love. He is the only One who can fill your need.

In the name of Jesus Christ,
>   I bless your spirit with Love.
God is love—the essence of love:
>   Love lives in you—
>   you live in Love.
Receive His love and love Him in return,
>   and love all that He loves.

I bless you with an exchange—
>   fear for love.
What do you fear?
>   Rejection?
>   Conflict?
>   Being out of control?

Being wrong?

You have not been given a spirit
    of timidity or fear.
Love banishes crippling fear—
    fear of death,
    fear of judgment.
There is no fear in love.

Accept Love when you fail—
    walk humbly before God,
    receive His courage and strength,
    live face to face with Him.

You were created
    with the Garden of Eden in mind:
    you were created for love and peace,
    for nurture and comfort,
    for friendship and companionship,
    for provision and protection.

Relinquish your requirement
    that a person or circumstance fulfill
    what you need.
Jesus is the only One
    who can give you what you need.

I bless you with boldness to take hold
    of what you have been given:
    unconditional love,
    disciplined thought patterns,
    understanding,

self-control,
good judgment,
right decisions,
safe thinking,
power and authority.

Stir up the gifts imparted to you.
May you respond
 with simple steps of obedience
 and see God act on your behalf.

Blessing of Unrelenting Love

Psalm 103

In the name of Jesus Christ,
    I speak to your spirit
    to hear what the Spirit of the Lord is saying.
Today, remember God's miraculous kindness.
May you be fully satisfied in Him,
    and may the deepest recesses of your heart
    respond to His wondrous favor.

Make this prayer your very own:

My Soul blesses you, Lord:
You abundantly forgive every sin.
You rescued me from hell.
You saved my life.

My soul celebrates you, Lord:
You heal all of me, inside and out.
You cure all my diseases.
You mend my broken heart.
You anoint me with compassion.
You crown me with mercy.
You embrace me with goodness.
You restore me with your strength and beauty,
You renew me—to fly again.

My soul is satisfied in you, Lord:
You satisfy my desires with good things.

You defend me with justice.
You put me back on my feet.
You make things right.
You unveil your plans to me.
You show me how you work and what you do.

With my whole life I bless you, Lord:
You know me inside and out—
You didn't treat me the way I deserved.
You don't hold a grudge against me.
You don't get even with me for what I've done.
You kindly and tenderly father me.
You are forever patient with me when I fail.
You discipline me—as your child—for my sins.
You have removed my guilt—
as far as east is from west!

I live in awe of you, Lord:
Your mercy extends beyond the highest Heavens.
Your loyal love is grander than the glorious skies.
Your tenderness is overwhelming.
Your love is endless—eternal—
unbroken—unrelenting.

I am overwhelmed by you, Lord:
You are faithful to me.
You make things right again.
You faithfully keep every promise you make.
You pass your promises down to my children.
You pass your promises to the generations beyond—
if I will follow your ways and keep your word.

Holy God, all that is within me
bows in wonder and love:
Your eternal throne is strong and secure.
You are sovereign and rule the entire universe.
Your works celebrate you throughout your domain.
I will celebrate you and praise you, Lord —
with all my heart!

To all who follow in God's ways:
to all who listen to the voice of His word,
to all who keep His word,
to His mighty heroes—messengers of power,
to His mighty warriors—
ministers who serve Him well,
to His Kingdom—His creation—
the works of His hand,
may God be your heart and soul's celebration!

Bless the Lord!
Be blessed—fully satisfied—in God.

Blessing of God's Heartbeat
John 13:23; 20:2; 21:7, 20

In Jesus' time, people ate and conversed in a semi-reclining position, on mats or cushions. At one meal, while John was reclining next to Jesus, he leaned back on Jesus' chest and rested his head on the heart of God. John proclaimed his own identity as the "one whom Jesus loves."

In 2001, I experienced what it felt like to lay my head on Abba's heart and listen to His heartbeat. It was more than "knowing." It was an encounter. I bless you with receiving your true identity as you proclaim these words over yourself: "I am the one Jesus loves."

I bless you, in the name of Jesus Christ,
    with your true self.
Your primary identity is not:
    I am a man or *I am a woman,*
    I am a father or *I am a mother,*
    I am a minister, pastor, teacher, etc.
Your identity primarily is:
    I am the one Jesus loves.

May you lay your head on God's heart
    and listen to His heartbeat:
    be child-like,
    be held,
    confide in Him,
    remain in His embrace.

When you come to know Abba Father,
     you come to know yourself.
You were created in love, by Love, for love
     and you are the one He loves.

He does not love you the same
     as the millions of others throughout time.
His love is not impersonal:
     He does not compare you to another soul,
     His love is individual, intimate, personal.

He bestows His favor over you—
     can you hear His heart?
Who is waiting for intimacy more—you or Him?
Who loves more?
If you know the answer,
     why do you not come?
I bless you with coming to Jesus!

Blessing of Humility
John 21:3-7; Luke 22:31-34

I identify with Peter, and I want to have a heart like his. His story is my story; his testimony is my testimony. Peter's interactions with Jesus have inspired me to turn to Jesus as quickly as I can, especially when I see my failure and weakness. A fear-filled life—the fear of death or the fear of judgment—is crippling and reveals that I am not yet fully formed in love.

May you surrender your self-reliance and agree that you need God's love. Choose to receive it.

In the Name of Jesus Christ,
    I bless you with assurance of Love.
Fill your lungs with the rarified air of Heaven;
    breathe in to full capacity,
    and run to Jesus.

What did Peter see in Jesus?
What did he know that so many don't?
What was it about Jesus that inspired such trust?

A man stood on the shore and called out
    to those who had been fishing all night:

    Have you no food?
    Cast the net on the right side of the boat,
    and you will find some.

The disciples obeyed and the net filled with fish—

too many to haul in.
When Peter understood it was Jesus speaking,
    he dove into the sea,
    swimming to Him as fast as he could.

Peter was not afraid of Jesus.
He was not paralyzed by his past:
    a failure as a friend,
    a coward in crisis,
    a denier of Jesus.
Why did he not hold back in shame?

Be blessed with such humility of heart.
Jesus invites you:

> *I have prayed for you*
> *that your faith will not fail.*
> *When you return to me,*
> *encourage others with your story,*
> *strengthen them when they fail.*

I bless you with instantaneous turning.
Jesus has interceded for you
    that your faith should not fail,
    that you would turn and see Him,
    that you would return to Him.

Use your failure as the very catalyst to return,
    to entrust yourself to Him,
    to receive His love—
    and to love Him in return.

When you start to take matters into your own hands,
    return to God's original call.
When you have nothing to show for toiling all night,
    be guided by His voice.
When you start to give up on your dream,
    be responsive to His Spirit.

Jesus loves you when you are taking
    a lot of time to learn,
    and when you have to take the test again.
He enjoys you and loves you—
    during your weakness and failure.
He is delighted that you come
    and let Him love you.

I bless you with an open heart
    to receive the love of God.
Even when you live out the consequences
    of your actions, He protects you.
He nurtures you and covers your wounds.
He is not ashamed of you.
He is not embarrassed by you—
    nothing takes Him by surprise.

May you know God's heart for you.
You can fail and still be blessed—
    when you receive His comfort,
    when you receive His strength,
    when you receive His training for love.

I bless you with a childlike response—
    with a soft heart,

with simplicity of faith,
with arms wide open,
with running to Jesus.

Receive God's forgiveness
with no more regrets.
Don't waste your sorrow—
go and strengthen others.

Blessing of Destiny
John 21:9-17; Romans 4:16-17; Song of Songs 8:6-7

The last time Peter saw Jesus around a charcoal fire was the cold night he denied Jesus—for the third time. After the resurrection, Jesus appeared to His disciples. It was early morning on the seashore, also around a charcoal fire. Three times Peter confessed his love to Jesus. Three times, Jesus brought healing and restoration of Peter's destiny and calling.

I bless your spirit, in the Name of Jesus Christ,
    with realignment to your destiny:
    Jesus and you, together.

Be filled with full trust
    in your Maker and King.
The fulfillment of His promises for you
    are awaiting your reception—
    trust in Him,
    trust what He does,
    trust His way of doing things.

You cannot break what God promises.
Come into agreement with Him:
    His promise is a pure gift,
    His promise is secured,
    His promise is true.
Take hold of His promises and don't let go.

Your destiny is realized

not because you lived a life without failure,
not because you made something out of your life,
but because God made something out of you.

Dare to trust God
 to do what only He can do:
 giving life to the dead,
 calling into being what does not exist.

When everything seems hopeless,
 believe anyway!
May you refuse to live on the basis
 of what you cannot do.
Live by what God said *He* would do.

Receive the Father's love,
 especially at your point of greatest failure.
He has made a covenant with you—
 a holy promise, guaranteed.

Jesus asks:

> *Do you love me without condition?*
> *Do you burn with passion for me?*
> *Do you have affection for me?*
> *Do you love me when you don't understand?*
> *Do you love me even when you don't feel anything—*
> *when it hurts too much,*
> *when you don't feel safe?*
> *Do you love me, even when you fail me,*
> *deny me, betray me?*

What an astounding question from Jesus!
Do you hear the longing in His heart?
Do you hear His impassioned desire?
How could He risk such vulnerability—
    without much promise of return?
What kind of a love is this—
    God laying bare His heart?

The God of the universe lets you affect Him—
    His living, consuming flame
    seals you to His heart.
His passion for you is stronger
    than death and the grave.
Place His unrelenting fire of love
    over your whole being.

I bless you with sight.
Ready yourself for the hard questions—
    confront your frightening emptiness,
    come to the end of yourself,
    renounce self-hatred,
    and surrender to Love.

The love of Jesus Christ alone
    establishes status and confers dignity.
You receive authority based only
    on the love of Jesus.

Now, give away what you possess:
    love God with the love He gives you—
    love and care for others with His love.

Blessing of Finishing Well
John 21:18-22

Jesus prophesied Peter's future. Historical records tell us that Peter was crucified for his faith; he died a martyr. Historians also believed that Peter asked to be hung upside down—feeling unworthy of being crucified in the same way as his Messiah.

Jesus foretold Peter's death and told him he would finish well. Peter may have denied Jesus in the past, but he would not deny Him in the end.

I wonder what it would be like to have Jesus prophesy over me that I would love Him so much that my beliefs, thoughts, and actions would not deny Him? That I would finish well? When Holy Spirit highlighted this passage of Scripture in John 21, I was impacted deep in my core. I couldn't retell Peter's story without tears. I desire to finish well by loving well.

Be blessed, in the Name of Jesus Christ,
> with living well,
> with loving well,
> with finishing well.

When you were young,
> you went where you wanted to go,
> you did what you wanted to do.
I bless you with a turnaround.
May your life and death now glorify God!

Hear the voice of Jesus

inviting you to life—
Come follow me!

When you look around
to see what others are doing,
hear the words of Jesus:

What is that to you?
You follow me.

What is standing in your way of following?
Do you feel too young or too old?
Not gifted enough?
Alone, with no spouse?
Married, but not unified?
Too broken?
Without a place in the Church?
What is that to you? Follow Jesus.

What is standing in your way of following Him?
Are you protecting yourself from every slight?
Shielding yourself from bad opinion?
Cringing under every criticism?
Frustrated someone is preferred over you?
What is that to you? Follow Jesus.

Follow Jesus Christ, the Messiah;
step into your divine destiny—
be filled and empowered
by the Holy Spirit.
I bless you with speaking His words of life.
May those who hear you

marvel at the wonderful works of God.

I bless you with wholehearted devotion to Jesus,
and with hearing Him tell you
that you loved well,
that you finished well.

PART II:

BLESSINGS OF LOVE FROM SONG OF SONGS

Jesus, the Shepherd King, sings His song of passion for His Bride, the Church—a divine romance of true love. The blessings in this section were inspired by *Song of Songs: Divine Romance (Passion Translation)*, by Dr. Brian Simmons. He describes Song of Songs as an anointed allegory—a divine parable—of how Jesus makes His bride (the Shulamite) beautiful and holy by casting out her fear with His perfect love.

Because the original Hebrew text was written almost three thousand years ago, Dr. Simmons chose to translate the equivalent meaning of the words, not just the words. The name "Shulamite" and the word for Solomon are the same root word—one feminine, one masculine.

I was also inspired by the insight and wisdom in the book, *Song of the Bride*, by Jeanne Guyon. She lived from 1648-1717 and influenced the Church mightily. I discovered some of her writings in 1992, and she was the first to open my understanding of Song of Songs.

Simmons and Guyon not only gave me a wealth of understanding but—more importantly—a love for this ancient book. I incorporated what I learned from these two authors into the following blessings and the notes before them.

Some Bible translations say that Song of Songs is about a marriage of two people made "one flesh" (Genesis 2:24). Translating this passage as relating just to marriage provides only a faint image of the unity between God and the soul becoming "one spirit" (I Corinthians 6:17). *The Passion Translation* captures the true essence of this allegory.

I have been deeply impacted by this divine poem of romance—a picture of the suffering love of Jesus Christ dripping down from Calvary's tree, offered to every lover of God.

This poem has a place in my family heritage, as well. We are descendants of Sir Francis Quarles, an English poet who lived from 1592 to 1644. Over a decade ago, Anna found the following excerpt of one of his poems in an anthology. It is inspired by Song of Songs....

from My Beloved is Mine and I am His

Nor Time, nor Place, nor Chance, nor Death can bow
My least desires until the least remove;
He's firmly mine by Oath; I, His, by Vow;
He's mine by Faith, and I am His by Love;
He's mine by Water; I am His by Wine;
Thus I my Best-Beloved's am; thus He is mine.

He is my Altar; I, his Holy Place;
I am his Guest; and he, my living Food;
I'm his, by Penitence; He, mine by Grace;
I'm his, by Purchase; He is mine, by Blood.
He's my supporting Elm, and I, his Vine:
Thus I my Best-Beloved's am; thus He is mine.

He gives me wealth, I give him all my Vowes:
I give him songs; He gives me length of dayes:
With wreaths of Grace he crowns my conqu'ring brow
And I his Temples, with a Crowne of Praise;
Which he accepts as an ev'rlasting signe,
That I my Best-Beloved's am; that He is mine.

—Francis Quarles

Blessing of True Love
Song of Songs 1:1-4; Luke 17:21

The basis for all love is a covenant love. This blessing is to awaken desire for intimate life—a spiritual oneness with Jesus. He dwells in our spirit. We experience His embrace in our spirit and soul where the affections of our heart, our understanding of life, our memories, and our will reside.

The Hebrew word translated as "kisses of the mouth" defines a divine Spirit-kiss. Jesus is the Word; His word— His breath—is His divine kiss of love. By a creative act, He formed and breathed life into Adam at Creation—and with the same breath, Jesus breathed into the disciples, and they were reborn from above (John 20:22). His Word is the revelation of His love breathed into us. This word also can be translated "to equip" or "to arm for battle." We need an impartation of God's Word to call us to life and love. We need His Word to become trained and equipped warriors—overcomers.

I bless your spirit, in the name of Jesus Christ,
    to receive this impartation:
    receive God's breath of revelation,
    receive the divine kisses of His Word
    breathed into you,
    calling you to life and love—
    awakening your soul with song.

Receive His kind caresses—

His saving, forgiving, keeping embrace—
inviting you to intimate friendship
and comforting your heart
with tender loving-kindness.

The love of Jesus is sweeter
and more desirable than vintage wine—
intoxicating—yet quickening your senses,
reviving you, filling you.

Receive His divine Spirit-Kiss—His breath—
His word equipping you,
making you responsive and ready—
a warrior armed for battle.

You are in training to be an overcomer—
no longer a victim,
no longer running in fear,
no longer walling yourself off,
or shutting yourself down.

May you fight a good fight,
not out of self-preservation,
not from your own strength,
not in your own way,
but with the authority and power of God.
May you fight in the army of God,
under His weighty glory.

Be armed with the kiss of His love—
with His weapons,
focused on His directives,

moving at the sound of His command,
wielding the sword of His Word,
taking captive every thought
opposed to His truth.

May you be nourished
   with the sweetness of true love—
   the love of your Shepherd-King.

May this be your story and song:

   Jesus, your words are kisses—
   they are sweeter and better than vintage wine.
   I am intoxicated with your love.
   Your love is goodness and more goodness.
   Your presence is so pleasing—so fragrant.
   Your name is Flowing Oil—
   pure, poured-out oil—anointing me over and over.
   You draw me into your heart,
   you embrace me with kindness.
   Lead me out and we will run away together
   into the Holy of Holies—into your glory.

I bless you with intoxicating joy
   as you drink the fruit of His vine,
   celebrate His divine Spirit-kiss,
   and experience His encircling embrace.

Blessing of Beauty
Song of Songs 1:5-11

I bless your spirit with courage to overcome,
    in the name of Jesus Christ.
In the twilight darkness of your soul,
    may you break out of your isolation,
    your helplessness,
    your aimless wandering.

Though you are assaulted
    by the burning anger of others—
    cut off, ridiculed, alone, uncared for—
    you are not left out!

Live in the blessing of your covenant love,
    your shared communion,
    your oneness—with your Shepherd King.

Rest under His shade in the heat of the day.
Let no veil separate you from His extravagant love.
Long for Him, wrap yourself around Him,
    listen to His heartbeat.

May you let your heart be surrounded
    by His suffering love,
    His atoning, redeeming grace.
Be comforted by His anointing balm poured out—
    over and over upon you—
    curing your lonely heart.

As you experience the beauty and love of Jesus—
    His very name evoking song and music—
    I bless you with ears to hear Him
    speaking over you:

My radiant one—you are lovely.
If you lose sight of me, follow in my footsteps.
Bring your cares to me.
Bring your burdens to me.
Come to me and you will find me.
Let me tell you what I feel—how I see you.
To me, you are beauty itself.
Together, we will enhance your beauty,
making you holy and radiant.
We will mark you with our redeeming grace.

I bless you with the radiance of the Trinity—
    encircled in the love of the Father,
    the Son, and Holy Spirit—
    reflecting their glory.

Blessing of the Cross
Song of Songs 1:12-17; Psalm 57:7-11

Verse 13 speaks of a bundle of tied-up myrrh placed over the heart—an embalming spice associated with suffering that reveals a picture of the Cross.

I bless your spirit in all the seasons of life,
    in the name of Jesus Christ,
    with knowing how deeply cherished you are—
    you are enveloped with His redemptive grace.

May you see the revelation of your Beloved—
    His joy in seeing you set free,
    His suffering love on the Cross,
    like a bundle of myrrh placed over your heart,
    for the rest of your days.

Jesus holds you and identifies with your sorrow.
May the fragrance of your praise awaken the night
    until the morning breaks,
    until He turns your tears into dancing—
    both now and for all eternity.

Can you receive His words of love?
Listen to your Shepherd-King:

> *You are so lovely.*
> *Your eyes reveal to me*
> *that my suffering*
> *and the glory of the Cross*

is revealed to you.
You are beauty itself.

Jesus is pleasing beyond words—
 He is your resting place,
 He is your perfect home—
 peaceful, delightful,
 like a green meadow bathed in light.

I bless you with knowing completeness
 as you flourish
 in His anointing presence.

Blessing of True Identity
Song of Songs 2:1-3; Psalms 32:7; Zephaniah 3:17

The Hebrew word "Sharon" can be translated as "His song." You are the theme of His song.

My friend, Daniel, let me share the story of his death on the operating table from a botched surgery. He came back to life from what the doctors recorded as a clinical death. During the post-operation recovery period, he was racked with excruciating pain that no medication was able to touch.

In the midst of that pain, Daniel experienced a heavenly encounter. He found himself high up on a lookout, led by an angel or Holy Spirit—he was not sure. The breath-taking scene before him revealed a seemingly endless array of white-clad, glowing beings as far as his eye could see, all facing a radiant light in the far distance. God was the source of the light, and these beings were facing Him and worshipping Him in song.

Daniel's eyes were drawn to what appeared to be a myriad of teardrop lights lifting from below. He became aware that these lights were the prayers of God's people rising up from earth. Every time a prayer was "sounded" on earth, it manifested in Heaven as light. He watched as each light was incorporated into the great worship of Heaven, changing the sound. The change was subtle and sublime, but always, always complementing and blending into the overall soundscape. Each word of prayer had meaning and substance and became an integral part of the "song" playing. Each word was individual and yet also harmonized into the whole.

Daniel thought of a great orchestra conductor. The conductor knows every note in advance. He knows every instrument. He knows how everything fits together, and—as each instrument rises and falls—he is able to discern its part.

The worship Daniel heard was far beyond an earthly orchestra and infinite in its complexity. The Lord was and is able to hear the total song and each part—each instrument and added note. He hears every prayer in a great song—a marvelous song.

As he tried to absorb this encounter, Daniel experienced the peace of this glorious environment. He was completely pain-free and unaware of what he had left behind. He was told that he could join all that he saw before him, or he could open his eyes and return.

He struggled to open his eyes without fully understanding why. He opened his physical eyes and— more importantly—the eyes of his spirit. He understood that our prayers become part of Heaven's song. He knew that God hears each prayer, and each prayer has impact.

When sound reaches a certain apex, it transitions into light. What a beautiful thought that our words to God are transformed into light.

When I heard Daniel's story, I thought of Song of Songs and the Shepherd-King, who brought revelation to His Friend, His Love—His Church. In our communion and oneness with Him, we are the song He sings. He in turn, sings over us. We are His song and He is our song.

I bless your spirit, in the name of Jesus Christ,
    with discovering your true identity.
You are His *Rose of Sharon*—
    you are the theme of His song
    and He is yours.

He sings over you,
    quieting you with His love,
    overshadowing you,
    surrounding you with His songs
    of deliverance.

I bless you with ears of the Spirit
    to hear the songs He sings over you.
You are His delight,
    and He sings over you with great joy.
The Lord your God is with you—always:
    loving you, He invites you
    to believe in His love,
    to receive His love.

Jesus wore the crown of thorns
    to take away the curse of sin.
In the temple of your inner being,
    you have been made pure as a lily,
    washed in the Blood of the Lamb.

You are the Shepherd-King's companion—
    His friend.
May you rest with delight
    where His glory never fades—
    savoring the sweet fruit of His love,

dwelling safely in His protection,
blossoming under the shade of His presence.

Blessing of a Mystical Rest

Song of Songs 2:1-7; I John 4:16

The root of the Hebrew word for "rose" can mean "overshadowed, surrounded, covered." The Shepherd-King has to encourage us to remain at rest in His arms. Jeanne Guyon describes the first kind of rest; it is the initial embrace of Jesus in the garden of our hearts, touching our senses and purifying them. From this internal, mystical rest, He will then awaken us.

I bless your spirit, in the name of Jesus Christ,
    with true rest—
    found only in His embrace.

He has transported you into His Kingdom—
    into His house of wine, His home of joy.
I bless you with devotion—
    drinking so abundantly
    of His strong wine, the fruit of His Spirit,
    that you think only
    of your Beloved and His interests.

He has prepared a banquet for you,
    but His eyes feast on you.
He is looking at you with His
    relentless, divine love.

Can you feel His gaze on you?
Can you hear His song over you?
Can you see the colors of His brilliance

reflecting on you?
You are radiant!

May your longing for Jesus deepen
    as you struggle to contain His love,
    as you look for comfort.
May you be revived by more wine of His Spirit,
    and refreshed again with His promises.
May you accept His invitation to rest in true Love.

I bless you with inner resolve
    to receive and experience such love—
    a love so great, so sacrificial—
    a love that breaches your heart,
    piercing and healing you.

Be born up by His left hand of exceptional care—
    be embraced by His right hand of powerful love.
Dwell in God—for God is Love.

You have rested with confidence
    in the shade of your Beloved.
Now sleep in His arms—
    your head upon His heart,
    listening to His heartbeat for you.
Stay there.
Rest in this gentle slumber.
I bless you with this mystical, sacred rest.

Blessing of New Life
Song of Songs 2:8-14

This passage describes a soul who has become focused solely on God and who no longer needs to fear winter — the winter is past. In Him, the land of eternal spring is linked to summer and autumn. The heat of summer's passionate love does not interfere with the mildness, beauty, fragrance, and pleasure of spring or the autumn abundance of fruitful grapes on the vine.

I have gone through many winter seasons in the garden of my heart. Jesus is always there — sitting with me in my debris or walking with me and talking with me. Though I might look barren of foliage and flowers and fruit, my roots are growing deeper and multiplying.

From the winters of my soul, I am also being drawn deeper into God's higher reality, dwelling in Him where there is no fear of a winter season.

Can you hear the voice of your Shepherd-King?
Can you see Him?
I bless your spirit, in the name of Jesus Christ,
    with ears to hear and with eyes to see Him
    and His joys of love for you.

He has come to you gracefully, swiftly, mightily—
    no barrier separating Him from you.
He is close to you
    even where you hide,
    even when you don't see Him.
The One who loves you gazes into your soul

while He blossoms within your heart.

I bless you with new life springing up
    from the death of winter in your soul,
    from the frozen cold of a fearful heart,
    from dampened rains of imperfections,
    from overwhelming storms of sin.

Hear Him calling to you—
    calling you out of yourself,
    out of your natural gratifications.
He is awakening you
    to be found in Him alone.
Hear His invitation to you:

Come—hurry to me!
You have asked me to come to you
and I have come—to draw you to my heart.
I will lead you out.
You are ready to go with me.

The time of hiding is over and gone.
The barren winter of your bondage has ended—
do not fear that season again.
An outpouring rain of the Spirit
has soaked the earth,
refreshing you, preparing you.

Do you see breakthrough?
The season has changed.
The flowers are bright with color.
The lilacs are purpled and perfumed.

The cherry trees are blossoming.
The turtledoves are cooing—announcing:
It is harvest time!

It is now a season for singing.
The air fills with songs to awaken you—
to guide you to our land,
acquired for you by my redemption.

Can you discern this new day—
a day of destiny bursting open
with early blooming of my plans and purposes?
Now is the time!
Now is the time for change.
Now is the time of blossoming,
each flower's fragrance wafting
as if to say: "Change is in the air."

Now is the time to rise up, my companion,
my friend, and come away with me.
Run with me, come up higher.
I have hidden you in the cleft of the rock.
I am your place of hiddenness.
Rest here in my wounded side—I am your Rock.
Let me see your face and hear your voice.
I love to hear your voice in prayer.
My heart is captured by your eyes of worship.

Blessing of Surrender
Song of Songs 2:15-16

Song of Songs describes a journey of the heart that begins by seeking God within, where He dwells in our spirit. We must spend time in that interior place where we encounter God face to face. In that posture, we are able to face ourselves and be healed from a wounded, untrusting heart. As we behold Him more clearly, He begins to fill our view, and we turn away from self-reflection. We are turning away from and beyond ourselves, seeing less and less of ourselves, because we are seeing more of Jesus.

I bless your spirit, in the name of Jesus Christ,
  with His words of invitation:

> *Together, you and I*
> *press through any resistance,*
> *any hindrance to our relationship.*
> *Together, you and I*
> *will remove any threat*
> *to your budding, blossoming love.*

To any part of your heart
  where you no longer perceive Him,
  where you have no evidence of His presence,
  where you are clouded with unbelief,
  where you have no vision,
  where you fear a transitory love,
  where you cannot enjoy His love,
  I bless you with the capturing love of Jesus—

awakening your whole heart.

I bless you in the night watches—you and Jesus
    together in the garden of your heart.
I bless you with a new day springing to life,
    dispersing every shadow of fear.

May you know His love for you—
    that you are no longer separated from Him,
    your dwelling place is the Holy of Holies,
    He is yours, and in Him you have everything,
    because you delight in each other.

You are His song—
    may He be your song:

My Beloved is mine
and I am His.

Blessing of Encounter
Song of Songs 2:17, 3; Romans 8:18

This song tells of the Shepherd-King who has hidden Himself—not out of cruelty but out of love. If He had not "left," the soul would not seek beyond self and would never be lost in God.

A miracle happens in this seeming "absence" of God. So many times He tenderly invites me to rise up and follow Him. And so many times I have settled with knowing the contentment, peace, and tranquility of Him, and nothing could induce me to leave them to follow Him.

This second mention of sleep refers to a "mystical death." It is a dying to self. In this slumber, rest is bestowed on us. He calls us to life but waits for us to choose to awaken—to follow Him. It is a parable of a spiritual dying to self and to resurrection life.

In the name of Jesus Christ,
    I bless you with an awakening
    to your soul's true Love.
In your search for meaning in life,
    in your fear of vulnerability,
    in your holding back and waiting too long,
    in the ache of your heart,
    in the tossing, sleepless nights,
    I bless you with discovery.

Your Shepherd King will reveal
    your secret presumptions,
    even as He destroys them

out of His great love for you.

You cannot retain Him—you cannot lead Him:
    He came to you,
    He came to redeem you,
    He came to form a covenant love with you.
He will lead you—not the other way around.

Your Shepherd King has compassion on you—
    knowing your suffering,
    knowing your regrets for not following Him,
    knowing your search for Him.
Seek Him and you will find Him.

Even when feeble and faint,
    you are blessed with His mystical, sacred rest—
    held in His arms, lost in His love—
    until you are ready to rise up
    and be led by Him.

Come and feast your eyes on your King—
    His covenant of love,
    His redemptive journey.

He approaches in His wedding carriage,
    leading the procession
    in a cloud of golden glory—
    a canopy of His presence.
He is anointed with the sacred oil of His suffering.
He is fragrant with His mercy.
He is triumphant, mighty—
    defending you from every terror of the night.

Your King has made a mercy seat
    for you and Himself—
    a crimsoned loveseat that will not decay,
    where you and He sit together
    under a covering of love and mercy.

It is a day of overwhelming joy—
    a day of His great gladness—
    on the way to His wedding celebration!

Blessing of Simple Devotion

Song of Songs 4:1-6; Galatians 2:20; Philippians 3:7-10

Song of Songs is a portrait of covenant blessings—a full possession of the Promised Land. Your deepest need for authentic love is met in your relationship with Jesus, the Messiah.

I bless your spirit with devotion to Jesus Christ,
    with offering your whole heart to the One
    who has made a covenant with you—
    an enduring love covenant,
    a love of pure authenticity,
    a dependable relationship,
    a permanent oneness in Love.
Jesus will meet your deepest needs.

I bless you with passion-filled love—
    a reflection of His graces.
May you have ears to hear His voice.
Receive His heart-felt words:

    My beloved, my friend—
    to me, you are beauty itself.
    I see you seeing me.
    I see your focus on me.
    I see your devotion and sincerity.

    You have received my love
    and my scarlet sacrifice of mercy.
    When I look at you, I see your offering

of sacrificial love in return.

I see you have tasted my word —
your life made clean and pure.
You display truth.
You speak mercy and grace
in a language that speaks only to me.
What pleasure you bring me.

I see your readiness to move at my word.
Your inner strength is stately and strong —
secure as a fortress.
I see your virtues and grace,
your pure faith,
your love resting over your heart.
I see your nurturing care for others.
When I look at you, I see your passion for me.

Instead of suffering alone without resolution,
may you join with your Shepherd-King,
allowing Him to embrace you
and share your sufferings together—united—
held in His winning might.

May you settle it in your heart, once and for all,
to follow Jesus as His co-crucified partner,
to the mountain of His suffering love.
I bless you with such love—
a love of passion found only through Calvary.

When you experience death—
of your self-determination,

of your right to yourself,
of your ways of making life work without God—
you will experience Life.

In spite of darkness, shadows, and fears—
before the dawn has fully come,
before the promise is fully realized,
before full breakthrough and healing—
hope in God.

With care and consideration, by the timing
and design of the Holy Spirit,
welcome every heart-wrenching memory:
every uncomfortable thought,
every stinging rejection,
every despairing tear,
every gripping regret,
every crushing accusation,
every bruising betrayal.
In all of these, be embraced
and united with Him—in His suffering.
Receive His wholeness—
experience full reconciliation,
and resurrection to fullness of life.

Go with Jesus to the mountaintop—
exchange your gifts for His Spirit–gifts,
exchange your voice for His voice,
exchange your influence for His influence,
exchange your own beauty,
in order to possess true beauty.

Blessing of Yes
Song of Songs 4:7-8

The Dictionary of Scripture Proper Names, *by J.B. Jackson, explains that "the crest of Amana" is translated into the English word, "amen" or "faith." It describes the realm where God's promises are securely kept and realized. It is the place where you are seated on high in Jesus Christ.*

I bless you, in the name of Jesus Christ,
    with reception to these passionate words
    from your King, your Friend, your Beloved:

    You are made ready, bride of the mountains—
    beautiful, flawless,
    seated on high with me.
    Come with me to our summit,
    to our sanctuary,
    through the "archway of trust."

    Look all around and survey with me
    all the blessings contained in Heaven—
    blessings of my promises.

    All my promises are yes:
    My promises are real.
    My promises are kept secure and settled.
    My promises supersede your earthly reality,
    My promises await your faith—
    your amen—your yes.

Blessing of His Passion I
Song of Songs 4:8-11

The Shepherd-King's response of impassioned love for you is beyond description. He is held captive by your love. The words He speaks in this blessing are in the context of seeing you in your struggle with demons, darkness, persecution, betrayal, disappointment, and sorrow.

When you experience such difficulties and still continue to worship the Father from your heart, it touches Him profoundly. In Heaven, the glory is so great that all will be compelled to worship Him. The Father is deeply moved when you worship here on earth simply out of love and joy for Him. When you worship in the middle of a personal struggle or battle, you touch His heart like nothing else. When you are in a dark place and you still choose to worship Him, He is overcome by one glance from you.

Living on earth is a unique circumstance; we will not be able to worship this way again. Allow yourself to be embraced in your hardships—your winter seasons. Be face to face with Jesus and see the look in His eyes when He sees your love.

I bless your spirit, in the name of Jesus Christ,
    with His overwhelmingly passionate love,
    by His heart that is moved so deeply—
    overcome by your love and joy of the Father.

While in the middle of the struggle and the battle,
    while experiencing severe trials—

beaten down and in darkness,
with no glory shining through—
you have held true,
still worshipping God from your heart.

Jesus invites you to join Him—
to accept His impassioned response to you:

Come up higher with me.
Together, you and I will wage war.
Together, we will deal with demons,
persecution, betrayal, disappointment, sorrow.
Together, I will heal your broken heart.
Together, we have victory.

You have reached into my heart
and—with a single glance—
have undone me with your love.
A gaze from your worshipping eyes
and I am overcome.

You have stolen my heart, my beloved,
my equal, my spouse.
I am held captive by your love
and by the graces of righteousness on you—
divine jewels—stunning, priceless, brilliant.

You are so satisfying to me, my equal, my spouse.
Your love is thrilling—
better than my finest, rarest wine.
The Promised Land flows within you,
releasing the taste of milk and honey—through

your loving words.
Your praises are an exotic perfume.
Your worshiping love surrounds you with fragrance.

Blessing of His Passion II
Song of Songs 4:8

Garris and I pastored our first church in the northern reaches of Montana in the Rockies. The climate there is similar to Alaska during the long, cold winters.

We discovered a special cherry orchard known throughout the region for its rich, sweet fruit. Because of the intense winters, the trees' roots had to go deeper than usual.

Those cherry trees appear dead in the winter, but they are more alive in their essentials as they become more firmly established in the source of their life. Their exterior is not being worked on so that the sap is not uselessly expended. The sap concentrates its strength on the roots, creating new ones and strengthening and nourishing the old ones—forcing them even deeper into the soil.

During the other seasons of their life cycle, the trees employ the whole force of their sap to rise into limbs and leaves, flowers and fruit.

Just like a cherry tree in winter, you've seen yourself stripped and barren looking. You no longer see the vivid green leaves that covered the irregularities and defects that had been there all along. In fact, you are not deprived. You have not lost advantage or ground. You may even look like you are dying, but what is visible can be different from reality.

If you are in a winter season, I want to impart this blessing to you.

I bless your spirit, in the name of Jesus Christ,
    here in the garden of your heart,
    here where Jesus meets with you
    and talks with you,
    here where He plants, tends,
    prunes, cultivates,
    and produces the fruit of His Spirit.

I bless you with extraordinary encounters with God
    through impartation
    and sudden breakthrough.
I bless you in the healing process,
    through a gradual growth
    and depth of maturity.

I bless you with the character
    needed to sustain you,
    built through a season of dormancy—
    with inner strength formed in winter's blizzards.

Your winter does not define your future,
    but it does nourish, help sustain,
    and produce growth for your future—
    its melting, snowy, spring run-offs
    quenching your thirst.

I bless you with new life springing up
    from the death of winter.
I bless you with the nourishment necessary
    to defrost a frozen, fearful heart,
    to clear the clouds of oppression and depression,
    to warm the lonely, long hours of darkness,

to awaken you from dormancy,
to take you into the next season of growth
and cause you to bloom.

Blessing of Fruit
Song of Songs 4:12-15

I bless your spirit, in the name of Jesus Christ,
    with the fruit of a soft, yielded heart.
Jesus is like oil from the olive press
    and wine from the grapevine
    flowing into your life—
    satisfying your parched heart.
May you flow back into the heart of God.

I bless you with ears to hear
    the King's song of passion to you:

My love, now that I have you,
I have secured you to my heart.
You are a secret garden I alone can enter —
a hidden spring,
a bubbling fountain,
a perfect companion to me.

Your inner life is a fruitful garden,
unfolding into a paradise of promise.
Your nearness releases aromas
of fine spice and ripe fruit —
fruit of heavenly passion,
fruit of mercy,
fruit of the light of my presence,
fruit of the costly, fragrant perfume of love,
fruit of redemption,
fruit of the fragrance of holiness,

fruit of incense in the Holy Place,
fruit of my suffering love dripping from Calvary's tree,
fruit of my healing balm.

Your life flows into mine.
Living water wells up from within you,
pure as a garden spring,
and flows into my heart like a mountain brook.

Blessing of Awakening

Song of Songs 4:16; Matthew 11:28

I bless your spirit, in the name of Jesus Christ,
    with the awakening breath of His Spirit
    blowing upon your life until you are fully His,
    stirring up the sweet fragrance
    of His life in you.

Invite Jesus to walk with you
    and talk with you
    as He did with Adam and Eve
    in His paradise garden.
You are now the garden He dwells in—
    may you yield fully to Him,
    may He taste the fruit of His life in you.

God is releasing the wind of His Spirit—
    His word breathed into you
    to empower you,
    to raise you up,
    to prepare you,
    to release you into full living.

Where you are stagnant, unproductive,
    and unable to move forward,
    I bless you with His wind in your sails:
    He is working behind the scenes,
    He has a plan to bring the support you need,
    He is releasing His wind of provision,
    His wind of peace.

If you are spiritually fatigued,
    if you are exhausted, soul and body,
    if your breath has been knocked out of you,
    be resuscitated by the breath of God.

I bless you with new levels of insight—
    clarity of vision,
    new understanding and wisdom,
    flexibility and great expectation.
I bless you with focused perseverance—
    staying on course and not giving up.
What appears negative, God will use for good.

I bless you with God's breath of refreshing—
    fly with His wind at your back,
    ride the slipstream of the Spirit,
    listen and respond to the words of Jesus:

    Come to me—get away with me.
    Come and you will recover your life.

By the breath of God,
    I bless you with alignment
    as He shifts you into a new place.
He is going before you,
    moving things into order,
    removing any obstacle.

I bless you with the wind of the Spirit,
    awakening your passion,
    and bringing dormant things to life.

Do only those things God is breathing on.
Receive His anointing to do great exploits.
Move in a new dimension of signs and wonders—
    be a sign and a wonder.
Take dominion over the kingdom of darkness
    and the powers of the enemy.

May you give Jesus full permission—
    sparing nothing—
    as He makes *you* His fruitful garden.
Hold nothing back until you are fully His—
    until His fragrance is released in you.

Blessing of Alignment
Song of Songs 5:1; II Corinthians 2:14-15

Listen to Jesus, your Shepherd King:

My equal, my spouse—
I have come to you—
you are my paradise garden.

I have gathered from the garden of your heart
all my sacred spices—even my myrrh of suffering.
I have savored my wine within you.
I have tasted the sweetness of the honeycomb
and all the fruits of my life in you.
I love what you yielded to me.
I take great pleasure in you—
enjoying you, delighting in you.

Now, dressed in all my beauty,
come celebrate with me—
raise your glass to love and life!

Offer up the fruit of my Spirit.
Because of my life in you,
you are a feast to the nations,
you bring good cheer to others,
you overflow with the wine of my life,
you carry my fragrance into every place.

You are celebrating with the King—
you and He—together!

May you be a feast to the nations—
    offering His wine and fruit.

I bless you with His words of life—
    His divine Spirit-kisses
    flowing through you to the world.
Declare and prophesy,
    bless and encourage others with His word.
God breathes into His word,
    and all things align with that word.

Blessing of Heavenly Dreams

Song of Songs 5:2-5

*The Shulamite has a troubled dream that her Beloved has
left her. The message of the dream reveals that He had
only withdrawn from her line of sight because of her
delayed response to Him.*

I bless your spirit, in the name of Jesus Christ,
　　with heavenly dreams.
Even though you let your devotion slumber,
　　your heart has been awakened
　　to His melody of love.
In the darkness of the night,
　　you hear His knock on your heart's door—
　　you hear His plea:

> *Awaken, rise up!*
> *There is no one but you, my love.*
> *You are my perfect companion and partner.*
> *Will you open your heart even deeper to me?*
> *Will you receive me?*
> *Will you come be with me?*
> *I have spent myself interceding for you*
> *throughout the dark night of Gethsemane.*
> *My tears and my heaviness*
> *are more than I can bear.*

I bless you with hearing His call
　　that stirs the deepest recesses of your heart,
　　even as you struggle to respond,

even as you question:

what more do I possibly have to give Him —
what more of myself would He find of value?

You have laid aside your own garments
  of self-righteousness.
You are now clothed in His garments
  of true righteousness.
You have given Him your heart.
You have been forgiven—cleansed.
You have experienced His kindness.
You have come so far—what more is required?

Yet Jesus calls to you—inviting you
  to unlock your heart at your very core.
He longs for more of you—and more for you.
May your spirit awaken—
  your heart rising up to meet with Him.

I bless you with surrender—
  drawn to the fragrance of His suffering love,
  your soul melting at His voice,
  your spirit trembling at His touch.

Blessing in the Night
Song of Songs 5:6-8; Isaiah 53:3-12; Acts 2:22-36

Sometimes, you think issues are fully dealt with, and then they reappear. You recognize again your rebellious thoughts and your natural defects. Sometimes, you suffer on every side, bearing slander, betrayal, dishonor, and persecutions from others. In these times, you are experiencing death to the self-life. You are invited to open your heart deeper to God who will make use of what John of the Cross called "the dark night of the soul."

We are already aware of our tendency to resist absolute abandonment to God, but we aren't always aware of the difference between voluntary resistance and natural resistance. The first puts a stop to the work of God, who then will not violate our freedom of will. The second has to do with our will, but is not voluntary. Instead, it is a resistance of nature. We naturally resist the destruction of the self-life.

Jeanne Guyon wrote that many are content to bear the Cross, but there is scarcely a single one who is willing to bear its infamy. Are we willing to "bear its infamy?" This blessing is for those times when you experience loss of reputation, disgrace, or humiliation.

I bless your spirit with absolute abandonment,
    in the name of Jesus Christ,
    as you take in the fragrance
    of His suffering love
    in the garden of Gethsemane.

Jesus is acquainted with your sorrow and grief—
    it was your pain He carried,
    it was your sin that tore and crushed Him.
He carried everything that is wrong with you:
    He was bruised to heal you,
    He was tortured and beaten bloody—
    travailing in His soul—to free you,
    He took all the punishment unto death,
    to bring you life.

I speak to any part of your heart
    that lies hidden away,
    closed and cut off:
    I bless you with impartation—
    a longing and desire for Jesus,
    a knowing that you were created
    for so much more.

Any delay is formed by your independence—
    your right to yourself,
    your temperament,
    your hasty behavior,
    your impulsive words,
    your self-preservation,
    your rebellion.

Where you have been deeply wounded
    and suffered loss,
    where you were struck and bruised
    by the violent actions of others,
    I bless you with God's balm of healing.

Where you were diminished, stripped,
and your heart torn, I bless you with courage.
May you acknowledge any refuge for your soul
that would keep you in your self-life:
critical judgments,
illusions of self-sufficiency,
avoidance of pain at all cost,
self-hatred,
a sense of superiority,
vows of self-protection,
dependence on yourself,
wrong alliances of dependence on others.

When you ask, *God, why are you not responding?*
My soul is miserable—
and your heart is torn with longing for Him,
you seek His presence but don't find Him,
you call out to Him but hear no answer,
who do you turn to?
Do you look to yourself?
Do you look to others?

Fearing you are defiled by human desires,
confusion and shame surface:
you feel tainted,
you feel unworthy,
you feel alone—suspended,
distanced from God and people.

May you be pierced to your core
with the relentless love of God:
He understands your weakness,

He sees your resistance to Him,
He knows you are unaware of other attachments,
or are aware but unable to effect change.

He sees your unbelief, your determinations,
    your judgments, your self-curses.
He sees where you have come from,
    what you have been through,
    what has been handed to you,
    what has been done to you,
    what holds you back.

Your Shepherd-King is right there with you,
    knowing that despite your rebellion—
    despite your fear of suffering and surrender—
    you have willed your heart
    to be abandoned to Him.

May you not be turned aside:
    repent of your independence,
    return to your first Love,
    long for Him,
    call out to Him,
    endure all for Him,
    remember the delight of His presence,
    search for Him and you will find Him.

I bless you with a heart pierced with His love.
I bless you with a mighty love for Jesus—
    a love persevering through all obstacles,
    through all disasters.

May you be filled to overflowing,
 speaking always of Him,
 declaring your love—
 a love so constant,
 so beautiful,
 so faithful,
 as to be astounding to Him.

Blessing of Holy Desire
Song of Songs 5:9-16

I bless your spirit, in the name of Jesus Christ,
   with holy desire.
Others will wonder and question such love:
   How can you care so deeply?
   Surely someone else will steal your heart away.
   Why is Jesus better than anyone else?
   What is it about Him?

I bless you with declarations of love!

Jesus, you alone are my Beloved,
my Shepherd-King.
You shine with such splendor—
brilliant yet so approachable.
You are without equal—above all others.
You lead with dignity, full of glory.
To be led by you is divine.
Your insights are free of distortion and full of beauty.
You see the fullness of revelation
with pure understanding.

No one speaks like you do—
so gentle and full of emotion,
so anointed, so piercing with your suffering love
and with your healing balm.

You hold unlimited power,
but you don't use it in anger.

You are always holy—displaying your glory.
Your innermost place is infused
with light-filled beauty.
You are covered in majesty—magnificent and noble.

All will be amazed by you!
You are steadfast in all you do.
Your ways are righteous—truthful and holy.
No one can rival you!

Why do I love you, Jesus?
Your whispers of love are the sweetest.
Your words are kisses—you are altogether lovely.
You are delightful in every way.
There is none like you—you are perfect.
Though I try, I am unable to express the inexpressible.
You fill me with holy desire.
You are my Friend—my Beloved—forever.

Judge for yourself—taste and see that He is good.
Be blessed with His desires—
　　Jesus is the desire of all the nations,
　　and you share in His greatness!

Blessing of Wholehearted Worship

Song of Songs 6:1-3; John 14:20

Be blessed, in the name of Jesus Christ,
    with a heart abandoned wholly to Him—
    with love so tangible that others long for Him
    and desire to seek Him with you—
    to know Him for themselves.

I bless you with delighting in Jesus—
    communing with Him
    as He walks within you
    in His garden of delight.

He is in your most interior center,
    your spirit—His dwelling place.
He feasts where His spices grow,
    taking pleasure in the fruit He has planted
    and cultivated in you.

Let all the harvest be for Him—
    desire His will,
    follow His leading,
    be His—without obstacle,
    hindrance, or restraint.

Free from self-praise,
    experiencing His goodness,
    may your song of worship be:

My Beloved is fully mine,
and now I am fully my Beloved's.

Blessing of Capturing Love
Song of Songs 6:4-10

Jesus is captured by you because you did not turn away from Him. In all your afflictions and humiliations, you did not look away from Him. In all your suffering and agony, you kept steady, increasing and deepening your love for Him.

Be blessed, in the name of Jesus Christ,
    with an all-consuming love
    in response to His heart for you.
You have captured His heart:
    you continue to remain faithful,
    you continue to press through the pain,
    you continue to declare the goodness of God,
    you continue to say *yes* to Him.

It is impossible for Him to love you too much.
May you hear and receive
    His words spoken over you—
    His response to your heart of love:

My friend — my love — when I see you,
I see a radiant city of dreams,
like the New Jerusalem where we will dwell
together in holy union.
You are more pleasing than any pleasure,
you give greatest delight —
you ravish my heart.

You are astonishing to behold —
like a banner'd army approaching —
even the angels stand in awe of you.
You have captured my heart.
I am overcome — undone — by the passion
I see in these eyes I adore.
I am unable to resist you.
I am overpowered by one glance.

You have yielded all of your being
in your undying devotion to me.
You have committed all things to me.
My truth shines through your spirit
with balance and completeness.
Hidden behind your humility,
I see the truth of your passion for me.
Others see you and call you blessed.

You are the perfect one for me —
made pure and innocent as the day you were born.
Look at you — growing up like the dawn,
moon-lovely, sun-radiant —
as ravishing as the galaxies of the night sky.

You are also ready for the fight.
Like a majestic army waving banners of victory,
you put to flight your enemies.
You are terrible and fearful to devils,
to sin, to self-love.
They fear you like they fear me,
since you and I are one in the Spirit.

I bless you as you stand side by side with Jesus—
  armed for battle,
  celebrating with each other,
  captured by each other's love.

Blessing of Single Vision
Song of Songs 6:11-13

The dance of love is literally "the dance of Mahanaim" or "the dance of two armies." It took place where two camps of angels gathered when Jacob returned to the Promised Land at Mahanaim, a memorial name in covenant history (Genesis 32:1-2).

I bless your spirit, in the name of Jesus Christ,
    with making Him your single focus—
    your eyes off yourself and on Him,
    your longings solely for Him.

When self seeks to intrude,
    you will be drawn to make decisions
    out of what appears to be right and reasonable—
    out of a longing to see if you are advancing,
    fruitful, flourishing—desiring to know
    if you are influencing others.

Instead, may your longings transport you,
    your divine desire elevate you.
May you suddenly
    find yourself seated with your King—
    your eyes only for Him,
    lifted up together!

In the presence of your King,
    surrounded by angels,
    restored to promise and inheritance,

dance a grace-filled dance,
a victory dance of love and peace.

Blessing of Redeeming Love

Song of Songs 7:1-9

*Saint Francis de Sales wrote that the fruit of the vine—
wine—is God's beverage. The fruit He produced in us is
made into wine, which then flows back into God. If a fluid
is poured into a vessel, it easily takes the shape of the
vessel, having no form of its own.*

*In its natural, self-willed state, the soul has its own set
form; it is obstinate and willful to the point of being stone
hard. Wood, iron, and stone must feel the fire, the wedge,
and the hammer to change their form. However, a heart
that is soft and yielding is called a melted or a liquefied
heart flowing into God—a heart able to be touched and
molded by Holy Spirit impressions.*

*The soul is also described as having stature like a palm
tree (verse 7). The female palm has two characteristics.
The more fruit it bears, the more upright it becomes. It
also will not bear fruit at all unless it is under the shadow
of the male palm tree. Life-giving water is found where
there are palm trees.*

*You cannot perform the slightest action by yourself
unless you do all things under the shadow of the
Bridegroom. The fruit you bear will not bend you toward
yourself; it will make you stand straighter under the
covering of His presence.*

I bless your spirit, in the name of Jesus Christ,
    with His redeeming love.
Dwelling in God, may you be reformed,
    wonderfully transformed, reshaped—

reflecting His holiness and beauty.

As the Shepherd-King speaks over you,
    may you be motivated by His proclamations
    in greater measure:

How beautiful — how graceful —
how dignified are your feet,
walking in my ways,
bringing endlessly good news.
Such royalty!
You are the poetry of God —
a living masterpiece.

From your inner being you overflow
with my Spirit.
You have become a birthing womb
for a generation of sons and daughters
nurtured by your graciousness and purity.

And like a tall tower, you have become
a shining light on a hill for the multitudes.
Your eyes are like pools of refreshing —
reflecting the light of God's mercy upon them.

Your strength comes from dwelling with me —
a tower of shelter from every danger,
a high place to watch for the enemy's advance.

You are royalty — crowned with redeeming love.
Your thoughts, your understanding,
your beliefs, your imaginations

are full of wisdom and life.

Your beauty transcends—
how you delight me!
Our love is my greatest joy.
Our garden of love is bountiful—
you are tall and strong, laden with fruit,
and the more fruit you bear,
the more upright you become.
Your words of love and sweetness
awaken those who are sleeping.

I will drink your love like wine
that flows unhindered into me.
Your resting, pliant, fluid love is transformed
and reformed in me—
assuming perfectly my exact shape.

Now I decree: I will hold you
with my powerful love,
possessing your whole being.
Your words are kisses of love
and my greatest delight.

Blessing of God's Desire
Song of Songs 7:10

I bless your spirit, in the name of Jesus Christ—
    be molded and formed in the Potter's hands.
May you be a vessel for His wine—
    the fruit of His love
    flowing unhindered into you.
May you be poured-out wine flowing into God.

No longer will you fear that you will be cast off
    or separated from Jesus—
    He will never turn you away:
    you are confirmed in Love forever,
    you are perfected by that same Love,
    you are changed into His likeness,
    you are united with Him.

I bless you with glorious participation
    in the immensity of God.
May you invite Jesus to conquer the world—
    you with Him, for Him.
There is no place too small.
There is no place too large.
Your place is in God Himself.
Wherever you are—you are in God.

May you declare without hesitation
    or qualification:

I am my Beloved's, and I am filled.

I am all the world to Him.
His desire is for me and fulfilled in me.

Blessing of Fullness
Song of Songs 7:11-13

*The Shulamite initially longs to see if the vineyards are
flourishing (6:11). Now—together with Jesus—they run
to the vineyards of His people to see if they are flourishing
and awakened.*

*This blessing is a picture of the Holy Spirit drenching
us with fragrance, passion, and beauty...and our response
to Him.*

I bless your spirit, in the name of Jesus Christ,
    with fullness.
Now that you see everything in God,
    you are filled with Him,
    and His desires are fulfilled in you.
You have given everything to Him.
You have consecrated everything for Him.

I bless you with both rest and action—
    not from your own influences,
    not from contemplating yourself—
    but by the power and influence of the Holy Spirit.

Now invite Him:

    To the One I love, come—
    we will run together
    to the forgotten places,
    to display your redeeming love.

We will discover if the vineyards of your people
are in full bloom and their passion awakened.

You have given all things to me,
and now I use them all for you.
I give you all my works,
my interests, my possessions —
all surrendered, all consecrated.

Like the beauty and sounds of spring —
the wildflowers in bloom,
the songbirds singing,
the fruit trees festive with flowers,
the love apples giving sweet fragrance,
the blushing pomegranates open with passion —
all comes from you and is for you, my Friend, my Love.

Every kind of pleasant fruit —
common and rare, preserved and fresh —
is found at our door.
All you have performed in me from the beginning —
all the new things you awaken in me each moment —
I have kept and saved for you.
All that I have, my Love, is yours —
all that is yours is mine.

Blessing of Enduring Rest
Song of Songs 8:1-4; 2:11-13

*The pomegranate symbolizes emotion and human passion.
It is a "blushing fruit" when opened. It is a fruit that
speaks of our passion for the One we love.*

*The third sleep is a state of rest — a lasting place of rest.
Deliverance from self creates an environment of such rest,
in which you are free to live wholly and fully for God.*

In the name of Jesus Christ,
    I bless your spirit
    with a deeper union with Him—
    always closer, always deeper—
    even though you are never apart.

May your passion for Jesus
    express itself outside and in.
I bless you with grace to freely
    and openly display your heart of love.
May you find such favor that others don't
    despise your passion. Instead,
    they are drawn to God's mercy and grace.

You were formed and birthed by divinity.
Jesus is your Brother and Bridegroom—
    both of you have been fed and nurtured
    by the Spirit of God.
Both of you are hidden in oneness with God.
You are made one with all that belongs to Him.

He carries you into your entire past, present, future,
     into your subconscious,
     into every corner of your heart,
     even to the place of your birth,
     where you once drew nourishment
     from a temporal, natural, human source.

May you open every part of your heart—
     all your family history,
     every memory good and bad,
     every place of injury,
     every place of shame or embarrassment,
     and experience perfect love
     in the communion of the Holy Trinity.

I bless you with the Word, Himself—
     speaking to you, instructing you,
     communicating by degrees—
     telling you the secrets of His heart.

He reveals truth in your inward parts.
He whispers purpose and destiny.
He transforms you from the inside.

I bless you with knowing every truth
     needed to enlarge your capacity for love.
Offer up to Jesus everything He offers you
     and all that He produces in you—
     the spiced wine, the new wine,
     the fruit of your love.

All of life is found in Him alone.

In this holy sanctuary formed by Him,
    no assaulting person or thing
    can touch you or affect you.
God's word is fulfilled:

> *The barren winter is past*
> *and your bondage has ended—*
> *do not fear that season again.*

Be blessed with the glory of God—
    for the glory of God.
Be blessed with His mighty protection
    and the perfect love of His embrace.
Be held by Him—
    and as you lean into His arms,
    I bless you with calm, enduring rest.

Blessing of Consuming Love
Song of Songs 8:5-7; Zechariah 2:5

I bless your spirit, in the name of Jesus Christ,
    with remembrance—with looking back—
    seeing how you walked out of the desert,
    clinging to your Beloved, your Friend—
    leaning on Him, your sole support.

You had no idea who your real Father was
    or who you belonged to.
Jesus raised you up and awakened you to life.
He delivered you and restored you—
    pure as before the Fall.

He awakened your innermost being—
    returning you to the grace of innocence.
He withdraws the venom from your soul.
He patiently heals you.

The Mighty Flame of the Lord Most Passionate
    is your Beloved, and you are His.
Receive His impassioned cry:

Fasten me as a seal of fire on your heart—forever.
No longer are you a prisoner to fear or death.
You are a secure, enclosed garden for me—
sealed in my love—by my living, consuming flame.

My passion is stronger than death and the grave.
My love is invincible—consuming you

by my burning heart.
I have enclosed your entire being
with my fierce, unrelenting fire.

Nothing can extinguish my flame of fire.
Rivers of pain and miseries cannot put it out—
persecution, afflictions, endless floods,
and distresses cannot drown my love.
My love cannot be bought or sold.
Nothing can quench my love that burns within you.

My fire stops at nothing
as you yield everything to me—
until you no longer think in terms of sacrifice,
until suffering turns to pure love.
Everything that belongs to me is in my safekeeping—
sealed up in our Oneness.

Blessing of Oneness
Song of Songs 8:8-14

May you grow up in Love,
   in the name of Jesus Christ—
   a love grown out of simplicity and oneness,
   a love becoming a tower of passion
   for your Beloved, your Friend, your Spouse,
   a love forming a firm wall of protection
   from your enemies of human reasoning,
   self-love, self-determination, and self-reliance.

May you become a strong wall
   of protection for others,
   guarding from harm those who
   are still little, tender, and vulnerable.
May they be blessed with God's graces—
   enclosed and protected,
   blessed with strength and beauty.

You have received God's favor.
I bless you with giving to others
   what has been given to you.
May you speak on God's behalf
   and enter the apostolic life—
   teaching others about His love
   and bringing Abba, Father great joy.

You are blessed in your simplicity of Oneness—
   one with your Beloved,
   your center,

your heart's garden.

From your vineyard of love,
   may you give all to Jesus.
Give double honor to others who serve Him—
   to those who have given their best to Him,
   and who have watched over your soul.

Hear the words of your Shepherd-King,
   your voice joining Him in song:

   Rise up!
   Come to me quickly, my beloved.
   Come dance with me.

   We will dance in the high place,
   on the mountains fragrant with spices—
   forever united as one!

A Memorial Blessing
Song of Songs 1:12-17; 2:3-7; 8:6-7

I wrote this for a beautiful, gracious lady at the memorial of her husband — the father of my childhood friends. Uncle Don (and his brother, Uncle Claude) married Garris and me 43 years ago. Uncle Don went Home at the age of 94. With love and prayers of comfort to Aunt Peggy and family:

I bless your spirit, in the name of Jesus Christ,
    with His comfort and with great expectation.
Jesus identifies with your sorrow:
    He is your resting place,
    He is your perfect home—peaceful, delightful,
    like a green meadow bathed in light.

You are surrounded by His suffering love,
    His atoning, redeeming grace,
    His anointing balm poured out upon you—
    curing your lonely heart.

I bless you in the night watches.
The fragrance of your praise awakens the night
    until the morning breaks,
    until He turns your weeping into dancing.
May you find fulfillment and completion
    as you flourish in His anointing presence.

I bless you as you rest with confidence
    under the shade of your Beloved—

your friend—Jesus.
Now sleep in His arms,
    your head upon His heart,
    listening to His heartbeat for you.
Stay there—rest in this gentle slumber.
I bless you with this mystical, sacred rest.

I bless you with these prophetic, passionate words
    spoken to you by the Shepherd-King, Jesus:

You are a secure, enclosed garden for me—
sealed by my living, consuming flame.
My passion is stronger than death and the grave;
My love is invincible—consuming you
by my burning heart.

Nothing can extinguish my flame of fire.
Rivers of pain and misery cannot put it out;
persecution, afflictions, endless floods
and distresses cannot drown my love.

My fire stops at nothing
as you yield everything to me—
until you no longer think in terms of sacrifice,
until suffering turns to pure love.
Everything that belongs to me
is in my safekeeping—
sealed up in our Oneness.

BLESSINGS FOR WARFARE

Much of Jesus' teaching and training demonstrated spiritual warfare. He taught His followers to live by divine wisdom: to be alert and cunning in the Spirit of the Lord. They were to respond in the opposite spirit to a worldly wisdom—a wrong spirit of shrewdness, cunning, deception, and evil.

Several years ago, an acquaintance wanted to meet with Garris and me to deliver a prophecy of great seriousness. It turned out to be a short word but prefaced with a lengthy forewarning, followed by a lengthy negative interpretation.

Although Garris and I only listened and did not comment, we knew that something was off about the prophecy. At the same time, we had no desire to be defensive. We would rather own something if it were true and let God reveal His interpretation and direction. There was no confirmation in my spirit about what was strongly being pronounced, but I felt a deep sadness. What if it was true, albeit unknown to us?

We simply listened, prayed at the end, and said that we would take the time to hear what God was saying to us.

Garris and I were not dismissive. We always want to inquire of the Lord. We did not want to make assumptions or be presumptive when it came to a word from God. True warnings or alerts can be lifesavers.

We asked ourselves: what was God saying, doing, and revealing to us? Was there something He was highlighting to us, regardless of whether the prophecy came in the form of judgment. Was there any truth spoken? What was God's truth? What was our response to be?

We had no grid about the word itself, but we knew the delivery and heart were wrong. In fact, it was the first and only time we have been given a judgmental and accusing "prophecy." The more we pondered and processed, the more it became clear how subtly manipulative and divisive it was, as well.

God gave His Church the gift of discerning of spirits—good or bad. When a word is given in the wrong spirit, we don't receive it from that person—even if they are right. In these cases, we only receive confirmation from Holy Spirit and trusted people.

Following the meeting, we took some time to listen for answers to our questions. I heard a Scripture in my spirit but dismissed it. The next morning, I heard it again and then again. When I finally checked it out, the answer was precise and clear. Over a period of several months, without searching it out, the same message was confirmed for us in more Scriptures.

God's word is sharp and concise. His words are divine Spirit-kisses, breathed into us. A prophetic word had been turned into a weapon of judgment formed from a bias and carried out by human reasoning.

Later, we discovered that this person had made accusations against us from our first meeting of introduction—pre-judging us from past, negative experiences with spiritual mothers and fathers who had broken trust long before we came into the picture.

We forgave and continued to bless this person and their family with healing, wholeness, and an outpouring of God's love. We also wrote to this person and communicated what we had heard from God. It was an invitation for open dialogue, but we never heard back. The prophets are subject to the prophets.

Every hit from the enemy becomes a place of testing and character building. These moments and events can become a breakthrough: a "suddenly" of the Holy Spirit, carrying a gift of wisdom, increased strength, peace, and so much more.

The Church is being trained to live without offense. We are in training to look only to God's opinion of us—remaining vulnerable and open and teachable toward those with whom we can have an appropriate trust.

God can get our attention through negative interactions. In such circumstances, we learn to be alert and more prepared for spiritual warfare. Some blessings in this section are the result of this story.

We are being armed for war. We are in training to become discreet and cautious, wary and shrewd, thoughtful and prudent, wise and cunning as a snake. And we are also to be inoffensive as a dove, harmless and innocent, without falsehood, simple and without mixture.

> *Wisdom is better than strength...Wisdom is better than weapons of war.*
> —Ecclesiastes 9:16,18 NAS

PART I:
BLESSINGS FOR WARFARE FROM MATTHEW

Blessing of God's Wisdom
Matthew 10:16; I Corinthians 3:18-19; II Corinthians 12:16

I bless your spirit, in the name of Jesus Christ,
     with spiritual weapons of warfare.
I bless you with these words of Jesus:

> *Be alert—stay alert!*
> *I have assigned you to hazardous work.*
> *You are deep in enemy territory—*
> *don't call attention to yourself.*
> *Be wise, discreet, cautious, shrewd, thoughtful,*
> *wary, prudent and cunning as a snake.*
>
> *Be inoffensive as a dove—*
> *harmless and innocent,*
> *without falsity,*
> *simple and without mixture.*

Don't be deceived by the wisdom of this age.
God catches the clever in their own craftiness,
     shrewdness, evil treachery,
     sly arrogance, deceptive scheming,
     and sophisticated cunning.
You are called to be the opposite of these.

The wisdom of this world is foolishness to God;
     don't be easily misled,
     entrapped in your own reasoning.
Instead of looking to find help

in human resources,
I bless you with divine wisdom.

Train to win!
I bless you with the skill to exhibit ingenuity:
 to be subtle, to be pleasing—
 attracting others to the light of truth.

May you be discerning with others—
 careful in your responses,
 prudent in your dealings,
 responding within appropriate boundaries.

I bless you with cunning and discretion
 to give and not to burden,
 to edify and not be offensive,
 to encourage and not position yourself
 for personal gain.

May you become an expert in thoughtfulness,
 circumspect in your speech.
I bless you with tactful diplomacy,
 with judicious insights,
 with strategic planning—
 sensitive to Holy Spirit leadings.

Be alert—be on guard!
I bless you with discernment
 concerning your treacherous foe.
Be carefully aware when:
 your heart hardens,
 your belief falters,

your love grows cold,
your relationships break down,
your discouragement takes hold.

May you learn the wisdom of God,
the ways of God,
the thoughts of God,
the heart of God.

Purified, you will see God.
I bless you with the likeness of an innocent dove:
live in the light,
live in honesty,
live in simplicity,
live inoffensively,
live without offense,
live single-mindedly,
live in peace as far as it is possible.

I bless you with living well—truly living.
Seek Wisdom, love Wisdom, walk with Wisdom.

Blessing of Inspired Words
Matthew 10:17-28

I bless you, in the name of Jesus Christ,
   with words inspired and empowered
   by the Spirit of God.
When you are in crisis—
   your motives impugned,
   your reputation smeared—
   don't be upset,
   don't worry.

Jesus said:

> *Without even knowing it,*
> *your accusers have just done you*
> *and me a favor.*
> *They have just given you a platform*
> *to preach my Good News.*
> *Don't worry about what you are to say*
> *or how you are to say it.*
> *It won't be you speaking;*
> *the Spirit of your Father*
> *will give you the right words.*

I bless you with influential ways of
   proclaiming God's unceasing love.
Don't quit, even when others
   respond with hate;
   don't give up!

You may have to flee their wrath,
    but be pleased to follow in the footsteps of Jesus
    as you endure to the end.

Don't be silenced, don't be intimidated—
    hear His words to you:

    I will whisper in your ear,
    I will reveal what is hidden,
    I will bring to light what is in the dark.

I bless you with boldness—
    don't live in fear of threats.
You might die a physical death,
    but your soul will live.

Eventually, everyone will know the truth.
I bless you with profound, eternal impact
    as you speak under the inspiration
    and anointing of God's Spirit.

Blessing of Influence
Matthew 10:29-42

From conception, our first concern is to look after ourselves. It is called survival. God gave you the instinct of fight or flight. But if you live your life in this emergency mode, you will discover you were never made to handle that kind of stress for very long.

You can spend a lifetime protecting yourself from every offense life can throw at you, and fear will increase. Spiritually, emotionally, and physically, you will start to dry up, seize up, and eventually "die." Living in an emergency mode will shorten your life. But what is worse, the life you live will not be what you were meant to live.

You were created for abundant life, and God is asking you to surrender to Him. Every time your heart wants to run, or shutdown and freeze, or harden and fight, exchange your self-preservation for God's protection. If your focus turns from yourself to Him and His Kingdom, you will truly live.

How much value do sparrows have?
Very little—yet not one falls to the ground
    without your heavenly Father knowing.
God cares about a simple sparrow—
    He cares about every bird, every species,
    in every spectrum of size
    with all their varied and magnificent colors.
How much more does He care about you?

I bless you, in the name of Jesus Christ,

with receiving God's attentive care
concerning every detail about you—
God knows every single one—
even the number of hairs on your head.

Because of your worth,
    don't let yourself be bullied!
May you stand up and be accounted for
    in God's Kingdom.

I bless you with courage to stand up for Jesus
    against world opinion.
The choices of your own freewill can
    restrict Him or authorize Him
    to stand up for you.
Give Him full authority—
    choose Him,
    and be blessed
    with His covering of protection.

Jesus did not come to make life
    comfortable and cozy.
Even good plans and traditions
    can be the enemy of the best.
Cut yourself free from arrangements,
    entanglements, expectations, and demands
    that have a hold on you.

Jesus said:

*If you stop living for yourself,
you will find me—*

and you will find yourself.

You and I are united.
Those who accept you
accept me.
Those who accept me
accept my Father who sent me.

When you accept a messenger of God,
it is as good as being God's messenger.
Even the smallest act of giving
and receiving in my name has impact.

I bless you with living in the greatness
of God's purpose and destiny.

Blessing of Mercy
Matthew 23:23; Micah 6:8; Zechariah 7:9

I bless you, in the name of Jesus Christ,
　　with the good that God has shown you—
　　and with goodness in how you live
　　and what you do.

God desires that you display mercy,
　　walk in His love,
　　and live with integrity.
I bless you with just and fair actions.
I bless you with a love for mercy—
　　mercy triumphs over judgment!

You don't earn His mercy,
　　you *receive* His mercy,
　　you *experience* His mercy,
　　you extend compassion
　　because of His mercy.

God desires mercy more than sacrifice:
　　His mercy is weighty and indescribable,
　　His mercy is kindness and unfailing love,
　　His mercy is tender and faithful.

You are blessed
　　when you dispense true justice,
　　when you practice kindness,
　　when you love mercy,
　　when you walk humbly with your God.

Blessing of Great Faith
Matthew 14:22-33; John 6:15-21; Mark 6:45-52

It is so easy to point out Peter's faltering confidence as he takes his eyes off Jesus and looks at the waves under his feet. Yet, who else do you know in all of history, apart from Jesus, who has walked on water? Even one? I always want to be the one who is willing to follow Jesus rather than giving in to my fear. To those who are in a storm: it takes a storm and a person who is willing to risk it all—to step out onto the waves—to encounter Jesus. Those acts will change history.

In the name of Jesus Christ,
    I bless you with great faith
    beyond the present,
    beyond the temporary,
    beyond the vale—
    extending to the Heavens!

In the darkness of night—
    in this crossing of your journey,
    as you battle contrary winds that churn the sea,
    Jesus is watching over you—
    watch for Him!

While you strain with all your might,
    laboring to maintain course,
    I bless you with sight of Jesus.

You are never alone and unprotected.

Jesus is watching over you,
    He is interceding for you,
    He will reveal Himself to you.
He may come to you in unexpected ways,
    beyond your scope of reality.

When you respond from the chaos of the moment—
    worn out by the all-night vigil,
    reacting in fear of the unknown—
    hear His words of invitation:
    Courage. It's me—don't be afraid.

I bless you with deep calling to deep—
    nothing holding you back—
    even if you are not sure it is Jesus,
    even when you have more questions
    than answers.

Let nothing keep you from Him.
Call out to Him:
    Jesus, if it is you, call me to come to you.
Listen for His invitation—*Come.*

With that one word, a whole new world
    has opened up to you.
You have been invited into greatness—
    greatness of faith,
    greatness of power in adversity,
    greatness of adventures in following Jesus.
I bless you with such heavenly encounters!

Exchange the strain and struggle

of preserving your life
for simple, spontaneous trust.
I bless you with new, child-like wonder,
    untouched by cynicism or skepticism.
I bless you with a restoration of dreams
    and imaginations—vistas of Heaven!

I bless you with courage birthed from Jesus,
    and the ability to clearly hear His voice.
You are not foolhardy
    as you step out upon the waves
    risking everything in response to Him.

If you take your eyes off Jesus
    and start to sink, He reaches out
    and takes you by the hand.
He honestly, yet tenderly responds,
    Why did you doubt me?

Faith is a glance away—
    He is right there,
    bringing stillness and peace
    as the winds die down
    and the storm ceases.
Marvel at Him—worship Him:
    Jesus, you truly are the Son of God!

With no more laboring,
    I bless you with a *suddenly* of the Spirit,
May you arrive at your destination
    speedily and straight away!

Love trains you in love—
   Love will never let you go.
Be blessed with boldness of faith
   when Jesus says—*Come!*

Let nothing hold you back.
Accept His invitation and go down in history
   as one who walks on water.

PART II:
BLESSINGS FOR WARFARE FROM PSALMS

Blessing of Refuge
Psalm 91

Psalm 91 took on special significance for Garris and me during a trip to Tirana, Albania in the late nineties. The country was in turmoil. A financial Ponzi Scheme had undermined scores of investors and devastated families. Our missionary friends, Chris and Laura Dakas, told us that rioting was breaking out in some cities. Mobs were attacking and burning government buildings.

That same weekend of our visit, we gathered at the local church: a large, rented room on the second floor of the main government building in Tirana. After the service, we stayed to say our goodbyes.

Suddenly, an explosion shook us, followed by what sounded like artillery. The noise turned out to be the massive, two-story, glass-plated windows of the downstairs lobby shattering from the impact of thrown rocks. A secretly planned crowd had gathered outside to vent their anger at the leaders of the country. They were prepared to destroy and burn anything they could, including the building where our church service had just concluded.

The remaining fifty or so of us could not get downstairs without using the wide, spiral staircase situated in full view of the blown-out windows facing the crowd. We did not know what the crowd's reaction would be, especially if they assumed we were working for the government. Our best solution was to not let our presence be known.

We waited, praying in small groups and individually.

We kept waiting and praying. (Garris and Chris, both ex-cops, were praying and strategizing!) Then we gathered in a circle around the perimeter of the room holding hands, while one of the leaders read Psalm 91.

Shortly after, plain-clothed government agents walked into the room and proceeded to take us to a narrow back stairwell no one knew about that led out the side of the building. We dispersed slowly, two by two, into the throngs of people, and made our way back to our lodgings. We had quite a celebratory meal that day.

Since then, every time I read Psalm 91, I think of that experience. It was far more serious than we had imagined. We found out about it as US news outlets reported the details, including an estimated 30,000 people who came to riot.

In eternity we will know how many times we have been protected from harm or death. That event was a clear experience of being "overshadowed" by the Almighty.

I bless your spirit, in the name of Jesus Christ,
    with refuge despite adverse
    or dangerous circumstances.

You are hidden in the strength of God—
    He is God on High,
    He is God the Destroyer of Enemies,
    He is God the Sufficient One,
    He is God the Nurturer of Babies,
    He is God the Almighty.

If this life is hard to believe in,
    and you find it hard to hold on,

begin blessing your spirit—
declare God's protection
as you endure the night:

God, you are my refuge.
You are the hope that holds me.
You are the stronghold to shelter me.
You are the only God for me.
You are my great confidence.
I put my trust in you, and I am safe.

I bless you with God's rescue
    from hidden traps of the enemy:
    He shields you from deadly hazards,
    He protects you from false accusation,
    He delivers you from any deadly curse,
    He deflects poisonous attacks.

God embraces you—His outstretched,
    massive arms surrounding you,
    safeguarding you.
You can run to Him and be hidden
    within His majestic covering.
His arms of faithfulness are a shield,
    fending off all harm.

You do not have to fear anything, day or night:
    not an attack of demonic forces,
    not evil launched against you,
    not prowling disease,
    not an everyday disaster.

God will keep you safe and secure,
  unscathed and unharmed,
  even in a calamity—
  whether natural or unnatural.

When you live your life on the mercy seat
  under the wings of the cherubim,
  under the shadow of the Most High God—
  your secret Hiding Place, your Refuge,
  your very own home—
  you will always be shielded from harm!

Evil cannot get through His door:
  How could evil prevail against you?
  He has ordered His angels to guard you
  wherever you go—defending you from all harm.

God's angels have special orders to be there for you;
  their job is to keep you from falling.
When you walk into a trap, they will catch you.
You will walk unscathed among the fiercest
  powers of darkness,
  trampling them under your feet.

I bless you with ears to hear God's voice:

  Because you delight in me and love me,
  I will protect you—I will set you in a high place.
  We will be face to face, safe and secure.
  I will answer your cry for help.
  You will find me when you are in trouble.
  You will feel my presence even in times of pressure.

I am your glorious Hero.
You will enjoy the fullness of my salvation
because of all that I do for you.
I will give you a feast,
and you will be satisfied with a full life.

Blessing of Fervent Love
Psalm 18:1-25; Hebrews 12:25-29

This Psalm contains a prophetic picture of Jesus hanging on the Cross crying out in agony. God heard David's cry, and He heard the Son of David—Jesus. At that moment, He shook the planet, bringing deliverance and triumph over death. David writes this song of worship when he is rescued from all his enemies. His response of love is a unique expression of passion—a word defined as an embrace, a touch or a hug.

I bless your spirit, in the name of Jesus Christ,
    with fervent love for God,
    your spirit embracing Him
    in response to His rescue.

Think of it—He is so real to you:
    He is your Bedrock and your Power,
    He is your Fortress and your Mountain of Hiding,
    He is your Pathway to Safety,
    He is your Tower where no one can reach you,
    He is your Strength and Shield around you,
    He is your Salvation and Light,
    He is your Champion.

I bless you with this prophecy of Jesus—
    answering your call for help
    and bringing you deliverance.
I bless you with His light piercing your darkness,
    your sobs piercing His heart.

Listen to His cry—the echo of your cry:

Like chains, the spirit of death binds me.
Horrendous torrents of destruction overwhelm me—
the earth is rocking and reeling,
the mountains are melting away.

God has turned His face to rescue you,
    His anger is kindled—
    burning on your behalf.
He has come to your defense,
    shaking the planet
    and covering the sun with thick clouds.

He reaches down into your darkness,
    rescues you out of your chaos,
    and draws you to Himself.
Though you are helpless,
    He takes you from your depth of despair.

When you are at your weakest and under attack:
    He rescues you,
    He holds on to you,
    His love breaks open a way,
    He brings you into a beautiful, safe place,
    He rewards you for doing what is right—
    all because He delights in you.

I bless you with revelation of Jesus.
May you receive His sacrificial love
    and follow Him in all His ways—

never stopping,
keeping your eyes focused on His true words,
obeying everything He tells you to do,
walking in the light,
surrendering to Him.
You are rewarded with blessings.

I bless you with the discovery of a great treasure:
when you deal with your sin
and keep your heart pure,
you give God a target for favor—
you will taste His goodness.
He loves to prove that He is true and loyal.

Blessing of Revelation

Psalm 18:26-50

In the name of Jesus Christ,
    I bless your spirit with Light.
May you exchange your earthly wisdom—
    your control and manipulation,
    your judgments and demands,
    your jealousy and division—
    for the wisdom of God.

God is shrewd toward the devious.
He will outwit the crooked and the cunning
    with His craftiness.
He disregards the proud and haughty.

May you walk humbly before God:
    He will turn on a floodlight for you,
    He will purify you,
    He will guide you,
    He will make you wise,
    He will watch over you,
    He will show you where to go,
    He is Revelation Light in your darkness.
    He illumines the path ahead with His brightness,
    advancing you through every stronghold
    that stands in your way.

I bless you with awestruck wonder of God:
    the path He gave you is perfect,
    His promises have proven true,

He is a secure shelter—you are hidden in Him,
wrapped in His protection.
He is your shield of grace.

There is not a more secure foundation
    to build your life on.
He has enveloped you in power.
In your worship, He trains you
    with weapons of warfare.

In Jesus, you have ascended
    to the heavenly places
    where you dwell in God's glory,
    and are made secure and strong.

Now descend into battle,
    empowered for victory—
    surrounded by His presence
    making you great.
You stand complete,
    ready to continue the fight.

The Almighty is alive and conquers all.
He has given you victory on every side.
Worship the unshakable God
    who rescues you,
    who lifts you up high out of reach of your enemy,
    who is merciful and kind to you,
    whose favor is upon you forever.

Blessing of Forgiveness
Psalm 32:1-7

I bless your spirit, in the name of Jesus Christ,
  with insight concerning the happiness
  and fulfillment that is yours.
Your rebellion has been forgiven,
  your sins are covered by the blood of Jesus.

He paid for your guilt and punishment,
  He removes hypocrisy from your heart,
  He wipes your slate clean.

Pause in God's presence—
  I bless you with Holy Spirit conviction.
Any dishonesty that you keep inside
  will devastate your inner life,
  fill you with frustration,
  cause you anguish and misery you can't suppress,
  give you pain that will never let up,
  sap your strength
  and dry your inner life like a spiritual drought.

In light of God's expressed mercy,
  receive the light of His truth,
  uncovering and exposing all
  that stands in opposition to Him.
You will experience forgiveness
  and freedom from pain and guilt.

May you experience this profound truth

of God's mercy—here in His presence.

As a result, you will be kept safe.
When you are threatened to be overwhelmed
    by the sudden storms of life,
    you will declare:

Jesus, you are my Hiding Place—
my breakthrough.
You protect me from troubles,
you surround me with songs of gladness,
you rescue me with shouts of joy!

Blessing of God's Leading

Psalm 32:8-11

I bless your spirit, in the name of Jesus Christ,
with these words from Abba Father:

> *I will stay with you,*
> *I will be close to you*
> *and instruct you*
> *along the pathway of your life.*
>
> *I will give you advice all along the way.*
> *I will guide you, leading you out.*
> *I will be face to face with you —*
> *leading you with my eyes.*
>
> *When I take you to places you have never been,*
> *don't dig in your heels and make it difficult —*
> *don't resist my pull,*
> *just come with me.*

I bless you with trust in God's forgiveness.
Because you came clean with Him,
    you will have joy and peace.

He surrounds you with His love;
    He shows you His kindness.
I bless you with celebration
    at the goodness of God.
Go ahead and shout for joy!

Blessing for Children

Psalm 8; Matthew 21:15-16; Hebrews 2:6-8

I wrote this blessing for a spiritual son and daughter about to give birth—and for their baby.

To the Parents:

In the name of Jesus Christ,
    I bless your spirit.
God has joined Heaven to earth;
    He has poured His heavenly glory
    upon you.

Be blessed with a glory sound—
    an infant cooing songs,
    a toddler shouting joy,
    a child praising God.

By the songs of your babies,
    God strengthens you.
Their praise rises up
    with the power to silence evil
    and to shut down opposition.

You are blessed with their worship—
    their wondrous, joyous, trusting,
    honest, simple, spontaneous worship.
Both the glory of the Heavens
    and the little mouth of your child
    reveal the majestic name of the Lord.

To the Child:

I speak to your child's spirit
   to hear what the Spirit of the Lord is saying:

   You are His masterpiece,
   you are crowned like kings and queens,
   you are glorious and magnificent,
   you are His image bearer.

Be blessed with the honor bestowed on you.
God's creative genius shines through you;
   be brilliant in His presence.

From the beginning, God placed the earth
   and all the created order under your feet.
Then Jesus redeemed you
   and delegated His authority to you.
All will be restored in the end,
   and you have a part in that restoration.

I call you to songs of deliverance:
   the dead raised to life,
   the blind to see,
   the lame to walk.
God validates you
   with gifts of His Spirit,
   with signs and miracles.
Out of your mouth
   will come the sound of Heaven,
   drowning out the enemy's voice.

You are blessed! God's heavenly glory
    streams down upon you—your life
    a living testimony of His majesty and power
    to all the generations after you.

PART III:
BLESSINGS FOR WARFARE FROM JAMES

To introduce the blessings from James, I wrote this confessional prayer concerning any negative and judgmental words we speak:

I confess to you, Jesus,
all words I have spoken
that oppose you and your truth.
Thank you for giving me sight
in identifying my negative,
judgmental, and destructive speech.

I renounce my agreement with the enemy
through spoken curses and self-curses,
through judgments and self-judgments,
through vows and negative, destructive words.

Lord Jesus, you have all authority and power,
and I speak in your name.
I command that all demonic spirits
and spiritual strongholds,
associated with my words of unbelief
be broken and rendered powerless and void.

I take back any authority given to the enemy —
spirit, soul, and body.

Jesus, I receive your mercy and forgiveness.
I receive from you
new ways of thinking and speaking.
I receive from you
a reformed and revived heart.

May the words of my mouth
and the meditation of my heart
honor you, Jesus.

Blessing of Maturity
James 1:2-8

In the name of Jesus Christ,
    I bless your spirit with endurance
    to grow into maturity.

When you face difficulties, tests, and challenges
    coming from all sides—
    consider it a gift.
That is the time to experience
    all the joy you can.

Untested faith is unreliable.
Faith is empowered under pressure,
    and when it passes the test,
    your endurance strengthens.

Don't try to get out of anything prematurely:
    let difficulty do its work—
    train for maturity and develop your spirit.

I bless you with a teachable heart in the process.
If you don't know what to do, ask God:
    He loves to give you wisdom,
    He is ready to give you wisdom,
    He *will* give you wisdom.

He doesn't scold you for your failures—
    for your lack of wisdom.
He overwhelms your failures

with His grace-filled generosity,
with His open hand of provision.

When you ask for wisdom,
keep your eyes fixed on God.
Stand guard over your thoughts and words;
acknowledge your discrepancies,
your independence,
your propensity to keep all options open
in case you need to rely on yourself.

Are you teaching God's grace to others,
but not receiving it for yourself?
Do you say, *God forgives,*
but also *I will never forgive myself*?
Have you put your trust in God
while continuing to worry?

I bless you with courage to identify your emotions
and behavior with an honest assessment of:
your unbelief, your indecision,
your disengaged, half-hearted,
restless, and wavering worries.

Jesus has set you free—
you are now in training to think free,
to live free—no longer a victim.
Fight on all fronts as directed by Holy Spirit:
Spirit, soul, body—in that order.

I bless you with stability in all your ways,
knowing that God

will do what only He can do.
May you contend for trust in God,
    even when you feel helpless,
    even when everything looks hopeless.

I bless you with belief in what God has decreed.
May you be:
    ready for God to act,
    diving into the promise He gave you,
    knowing that you will come up strong,
    sure that God will do what He says,
    trusting Him to make things right.

Blessing of Countless Blessings

James 1:12-17; Matthew 5:14-16

I bless your spirit, in the name of Jesus Christ,
    with countless blessings.
I bless you with strong faith,
    open to His goodness,
    even while surrounded by difficulties.

I bless you with true happiness
    that comes with passing the tests of life,
    training you for love—by Love.
True happiness comes because you love God.
You will receive the promise—
    the winning crown of life!

When you go through life's difficulties,
    don't ever say they come from God:
    He's not making life hard,
    He's not punishing you,
    He's not angry at you,
    He's not tempting you to prove He is right.
All evil comes from one source: the enemy.

God will not be tempted by evil,
    and He is never the source of temptation.
His Word of Life has power
    to continually deliver you
    from demonic activity.
He will save your soul.

When you are tempted,
    you are facing your own desires and thoughts
    that drag you into evil,
    that lure you away into darkness.
Evil desires become evil actions—
    and these actions can kill you.

So don't be fooled—
    don't agree with the enemy
    or give him a legal right to assault you,
    accuse you, and take you out.

I bless you with remarkable clarity.
God is the Father of Lights,
    and He shines down from Heaven upon you:
    He has no hidden shadow or darkness.
He has no wrong in Him—
    not even a hint of evil.
He is more beautiful and holy
    the more you get to know Him.

God blesses you with countless blessings—
    with gifts streaming down to you:
    gifts freely given,
    gifts good and perfect,
    gifts complete and wholesome,
    gifts sufficient and abundant.

God delights in you.
I bless you with blessings so innumerable
    they reach beyond you to others,
    spreading God's extravagant love far and wide.

Blessing of a Sensitive Spirit
James 1:19-27

In the name of Jesus Christ,
    I bless you with a sensitive spirit—
    able to absorb God's manifest presence
    embedded in your nature.

Take this to heart:
    be slow to anger but quick to listen.
Human anger is never a legitimate tool
    to promote the purposes of God.

Instead, listen to the Word of Life
    and respond to His Voice.
May His Word become like poetry
    written on your heart
    and fulfilled by your life.

I bless the ears of your spirit
    to hear the Word of truth.
But don't just hear and do nothing—
    you'll be worse off than before.
Hear and respond and obey.

Live out the message you hear:
    discover the reflection of God's face,
    perceive how He sees you,
    remember your divine origin,
    reflect your new nature,
    absorb the manifestation of God in you,

be continually delivered, filled
and empowered.

You are blessed when you gaze deeply
into the royal law of love,
into the law of freedom,
into the face of God.

You are blessed when you are drawn to truth,
when you respond to the truth you hear,
and you are strengthened by it.
You will experience God's blessing
in all that you do.

God will act when you obey.
What your enemy intended for evil
will become the place of your greatest victory.
If battered by abuse,
become a healed healer.
If verbally abused,
become a voice for the silenced.
If once homeless, orphaned, fatherless, comfortless,
become an advocate of compassion for others.
If once marked and tainted—
rise up in your royal lineage,
raising others up with you.

Listen to the Word of Life.
Speak words of life.
Bless others with words of life.

Blessing of Life-Giving Words
James 1:19; 26; 3:1-12; Proverbs 18:21

I will always be grateful to Peter Toth and his ministry Anazao *for training me in spiritual warfare. He taught me how to pray more specifically in the authority given me through Jesus. These Scriptures show us the seriousness and power of our words. When we speak words of death, we need to confess and renounce them.*

I bless you, in the name of Jesus Christ,
    with words of life,
    with prophecies of truth,
    with decrees from Heaven,
    with proclamations from the Word of Life.

I bless you with wisdom concerning
    the power of your words.
To be wise with your words
    is to be powerful enough to have dominion,
    to have self-control in every way,
    to be guided into full maturity,
    to be steered by character that is fully developed.

The words on your tongue carry great power:
    be quick to listen and slow to speak.
If you speak without self-control,
    your words are small flames
    setting a forest ablaze.

The tongue ignites fire:

it is the most dangerous part of the body,
it can create a world of wrongdoing,
it corrupts the whole body,
it passes through successive generations,
it is not easily overpowered and tamed,
it is fickle and unrestrained,
it is an evil toxic poison.

There is a spiritual law of the Kingdom
in operation, regardless
of understanding its full importance.
Your words are so weighty,
they carry the power
of life and death.
I bless you with life-giving words.

Blessing of Vigilance
James 4:6-10; I Peter 5:6-11

In the name of Jesus Christ,
    I bless you with vigilance.
Be awake! Be sober! Be alert!
You have an enemy prowling about.

Be on guard—don't submit to his enslavement,
    his torture, his bondage, his evil;
    be alert to withstand attacks,
    become self-disciplined in your responses,
    well-balanced in your thinking,
    and steady in your faith.

You are not alone in your suffering;
    there are many others going
    through hard times.
I bless you with an immovable foothold
    and a firm grip on your faith,
    knowing these hardships
    will not last forever.

May you submit under the weight of God's glory,
    surrendering to Him—your Hope of Glory,
    yielding to His glory in you,
    and seeing His strong hand upon you.

Be blessed mightily—living carefree
    before God—putting into His hands
    your anxiety over today,

your worries for the future,
your distractions,
your burdens,
your concerns.

He cares about every detail.
He is watchful over you.
He has great plans for you—
eternal and glorious plans.

Be blessed with living contentedly—
without putting on airs.
God resists your pride but continually
pours out more and more grace
when you are honest and humble.
Come closer and closer to God—
He is always close to you,
even when you don't perceive Him.

I bless you with surrendering to God,
submitting to one another,
supporting each other,
encouraging each other,
loving one another,
and living under the blessing of grace.

You are blessed with the God of all grace,
who is generous and who imparts blessings.
God's grace is His favor even in the middle of
your frustration, your fear, your suffering.

God made you complete.

He now works in you—training you
   in the ways of royalty.

I bless you with an outpouring of favor
   as you are united with Him,
   as He mends and repairs you,
   restores and prepares you,
   perfects you—matures you.

May you be established—
   turned in the right direction,
   resolutely, steadfastly set
   and confirmed to be on course.

I bless you with strength—invigorated
   in knowledge and power.
God is settling you on a strong foundation
   to build you up.

You are under God's power,
   authority, and sovereignty.
He truly has the last word.
Draw close to God and experience
   His closeness to you.

PART IV:
BLESSINGS FOR WARFARE FROM PROVERBS

To introduce the blessings from Proverbs, I asked my husband, Garris, to share this story.

When Hell Calls
by Garris Elkins

For four years in the 1990s, Jan and I lived in Berlin, Germany. We worked throughout Eastern Europe, strengthening and encouraging the churches in that region.

At one point, there was a stretch of several months when we received very unsettling phone calls in the middle of the night. When I answered the phone, a female voice would speak disturbing things in perfect English. I could hear other voices in the background.

When the first call came, I was so asleep and in shock that I simply hung up. At the second call, I knew these calls might be more than just pranks. The Lord gave me an assignment. He told me when the next call came to begin reciting Scripture and the promises He had spoken over my life. I was to do all of this in a calm and cheerful voice in the middle of the night.

When the third call came, I began to recite verses I had committed to memory. I spoke the promises of God I had received for my life. I did all of this in the dark of our bedroom as I listened to a group of people on the other end of the line laughing and mocking the words I spoke.

At call number four, I noticed a shift had taken place, and the time was much shorter. On the next call I answered the phone by saying, "I am so glad you called. I've been expecting you. I love to hear the Word of God and His promises over my life in the middle of the night." There was no response. The phone went dead and that was the end.

When darkness calls, you have two tremendous weapons at your disposal: the Word of God and the promises He has declared over your life. These weapons are empowered by God—not your maturity, the gifts you carry, or whether you are having a good or bad day.

For those phone calls, I knew that an argument, an emotional response, or an abrupt hang-up would not end them. Hell feeds on a response of frustration or denial. I needed to engage and speak truth. Truth is reality, and reality dispels illusion, bluffing, and lies.

If you are under attack, speak God's Word and His promises as your response to the voices assigned to assault your place of rest. At some point, those voices will stop calling because your words will become a tormenting sound to your enemy.

God's Word is powerful, sharper than a two-edged sword, able to pierce the darkness and illuminate the human heart. If another call came, I would call out God's promises of destiny over those on the other end of the line.

I remember when joy entered my heart in anticipation of the next call. The experience had become a display of God's goodness, and I gladly exchanged my sleep for the next demonstration of His power.

Blessing of Success
Proverbs 16:1-9

I bless your spirit, in the name of Jesus Christ,
    with a wholehearted trust in God.
I bless you with first things first:
    before you do anything,
    trust fully in God—follow Him,
    and your plans will succeed.
He will ultimately direct your steps;
    He will have the last word.

If you have elaborate plans for your life—
    for your career,
    for your future calling—
    don't put your trust in yourself,
    put your trust fully in God.

If you have stopped believing
    for a future and a hope
    and you have given up on life—
    settling for second-best—
    stop trusting in yourself
    and turn back to God.

Don't just be satisfied
    with what looks good
    or with what feels good—
    loving your own opinions,
    convinced they are correct.
God is with you, weighing every motive,

testing to see what is good.

You can count on pride
    to attract trouble;
    arrogance and pretense
    will result in adverse consequences.

May you avoid evil
    with its accompanying guilt
    and its grip on you—
    by the power of God,
    by His love and truth,
    by your responsive reverence for Him,
    by your acts of worship.

Before you make decisions,
    before you take action,
    before you do a thing,
    entrust yourself totally to God,
    and all your plans will succeed.

Rely on His directives.
Practice His presence.
Ask, listen, obey.

God made everything
    with a place and purpose—
    He can be trusted.
Your decision to put Him in charge
    will please Him because now,
    you have given Him permission
    to bless you—and He wants to bless you!

He will use everything
   to accomplish His purposes on the earth—
   even evil instigated by hell
   and perpetrated by mankind's agreement
   and participation.

He will use everything
   to accomplish His purposes in you and for you.
He will act on your behalf,
   He will activate grace
   to turn your enemies into friends.
He exercises His sovereignty
   to give you abundant mercy.

In making plans for your future, remember:
   God is the only one who gives you the ability
   to live out those plans.

Put your plan in the hands of Jesus—
   inviting Him to be in charge.
Hand Jesus all your cares.
Align your thoughts with His thoughts.
Agree to His will and ways.

I bless you with success:
   with success in relationships,
   with loving well,
   with finishing well.

I bless you with success in life—
   success in all that you put your hands to,

success in the steps you take to get there.

Blessing of a Good Leader
Proverbs 16:6, 10-20

I bless your spirit, in the name of Jesus Christ,
   with influential leadership:
   making God's work your work,
   His plans, your plans,
   His ways, your ways.

I bless you with true authority as a good leader—
   refusing to tolerate wrong-doing in your life.
I bless you with sound leadership
   built on a moral, righteous foundation of:
   cultivating honest speech,
   speaking with revelatory truth,
   taking care to make divine decisions,
   motivating without misleading or exploiting,
   acting with fairness in every business transaction.

I bless you with a love for godly counsel
   and with a love for those who tell you the truth.
If you listen to correction,
   you will be made wise—
   receive instruction and you will be prosperous.

Be warned: any overconfidence
   in your own efforts,
   any boasting in your self-determination—
   your skill and hard work,
   your status among the high and mighty—
   will result in a future failure.

Pride is a precursor to a fall
    and brings disgrace.
May you guard your ways
    and preserve your soul.
I bless you with spiritual authority
    sourced in a humble, yielded heart.

When you turn toward God,
    you continue forward
    on the highway of holiness—
    away from evil, chaos, trouble,
    confusion, and divisiveness.

Desire the wisdom of God,
    search for understanding
    and yield a greater return.
Make God your passion,
    and He will lead you to life.

I bless you with life-giving light
    streaming from you to others.
You will be like sunshine and spring rain,
    showering favor on those you lead,
    invigorating their lives.
When you trust in God
    you are blessed beyond belief!

Blessing of Divine Wisdom
Proverbs 16:16; 21-24

I bless your spirit with a wealth of wisdom,
   in the name of Jesus Christ.
Wisdom creates discernment;
   discernment enables you to speak graciously,
   and when you are gracious,
   your wisdom is better received.

I bless you with divine wisdom.
May you become a deep well of wisdom,
   sourced in an aquifer of living water,
   a fountain of life for others.

You are blessed when you trust in the Lord:
   He will set you on the right path,
   He knows the steps you need to take,
   He knows the obstacles to avoid,
   He knows your destination,
   He knows the perfect timing to get there.

I bless you with the insight of wisdom:
   with clear words,
   beautiful words,
   life-giving words—
   words that release sweetness to the soul,
   inner healing to the spirit,
   and energy for the body.

The worth of wisdom is far greater than gold;

a heart of understanding is better than silver,
and it yields a greater return.

Blessing of God's Plan
Proverbs 20:18; Isaiah 30:1-5

Be blessed with boldness
    in the name of Jesus Christ—
    a boldness tempered with carefulness,
    a boldness that is not arrogant,
    a boldness without flippancy,
    a boldness that is unwavering.

I bless you with a war plan:
    effective battle strategies
    prepared by consultation,
    directed by wise guidance,
    and confirmed by the Lord.

I bless you with a heart of submission.
Don't rebel and devise plans—
    charging into battle without wisdom,
    apart from Holy Spirit directives.

Ask His advise.
Take His counsel.
Put your trust in Him.
Strengthen yourself in Him.
Walk in His ways.

You will not be disappointed or shamed.
Your purposes will be accomplished—
    you will profit from your decisions,
    you will receive the help you need,

your plans will succeed.

What is your plan of attack
　　when you are betrayed,
　　when all hell breaks loose,
　　when evil is spoken about you,
　　when you are having a bad day,
　　when a panic button gets pushed,
　　when you are stuck,
　　when you have lost your way,
　　when you failed miserably?

Refuse to hear only what you want to hear.
Refuse false illusions and the desire
　　for only pleasant words.
I speak to your spirit; listen for
　　what the Spirit of the Lord is saying.
I bless you with a willingness to obey
　　all that God tells you.

Desire sight.
Discern deceit.
Seek truth.
Rely on God.
Love His Word.

If you have suffered greatly in the past,
　　with a well-meaning yet ineffective plan,
　　your defeat can be used as a setup
　　for your future victory.

With God's wisdom and might,

I bless you with breakthrough
for yourself, for your children,
for the generations to come—
for the Kingdom of God.

Blessing of Breakthrough
Proverbs 21:22

In 1994, Garris and I received a significant word. We were vacationing in "Carl's Cabin" on the Stillwater River a few miles outside of Absorokee, Montana. Early one morning, Garris heard these words from Holy Spirit: "My ability to lead you into truth is greater than the enemy's ability to lead you into error." Unknown to us at that time, we were going to make a life-changing decision to return to overseas mission's work.

We hung on to that beautiful truth through the emotional goodbyes to family and friends. It guided us through the upheaval of selling our home and most of our belongings—once again. Those words were imprinted on our hearts as we prepared to enter a new assignment that extended to the whole of Europe.

I bless your spirit, in the name of Jesus Christ,
    with an impartation
    in the power and authority
    of the Holy Spirit.

You are seated on High, in Christ,
    at the right hand of the Father—
    a warrior in training:
    training to overcome,
    training for wisdom,
    training to declare God's decrees.

As you step out in faith, hear this:

    God's ability to lead you into truth

is greater than the enemy's ability
to lead you into error.
God's ability to sustain you
is greater than the enemy's ability to destroy you.
God's ability to bring you life
is greater than the enemy's ability to bring you death.

From Heaven to earth,
    you will release regional breakthrough,
    you will demolish your enemy's
    strength of confidence
    and bring down his strongholds.

PART V:
GENERAL BLESSINGS FOR WARFARE

In 1988, I was in a serious head-on collision that could have easily taken my life. When I came to, I found myself in a hospital room with Jesus standing at my side. He spoke: "It was not your time. I am healing all." I had undergone an attack on my life. Everything I needed to experience in that moment—comfort, love, and protection—flowed from His presence and words. He had the timing of my life in His hands, and He would restore what was taken from me.

I later learned that though my body was bruised inside and out, my only major injury was a broken jaw. The doctors had wired my mouth shut so that my jawbone could heal. The head-on collision happened between my little Volkswagen Jetta and a large SUV pulling a trailer. My car was totaled. I did not have conscious memory of the impact, but I later learned of my rescue by emergency personnel who had used the Jaws of Life to extract me from the wreckage. My survival was a miracle.

From that encounter in the hospital and throughout the healing process, I felt an unusual sense of peace and wellbeing. It took a good while to recover. Even after returning home, I had to sip my meals from a straw for six weeks until the wires in my mouth were removed. My family would head off to work and school, and all I could do was rest. Instead of reading—which I loved to do—or watching some TV, I spent all my time enveloped in God's arms. It was He and I, together.

It wasn't until another car accident one wet and dark evening in 2001 that I gained a fuller understanding of spiritual warfare when it came to processing trauma. Though I didn't know it at the time of either accident—years and miles apart—both of them took place on sections of roads known to be accident-prone because of poor roadway markings and visibility.

For the second collision, a young lady ran a four-way stop, flying down the hill and through the intersection at high speed. I experienced the "perfect" accident. As she flashed by me, I only saw her car as a blur, inches from me. There had been no vehicle at the intersection when I looked around before proceeding ahead. I had pulled out just far enough to tap her in the "sweet spot" over her rear wheel. This swung her around to a full stop, facing the opposite direction she had been traveling. The damage was minimal to both cars. If I had started out into the intersection in a hurry and had covered just a fraction more ground, she would have plowed directly into my driver's side.

This accident was written up as a no-fault accident. It was her word against mine with no other witnesses. Before the police arrived, she had raged at me saying that she recently had been in another car accident and she was not going to take the blame for this one. Because I hit her, my insurance company did not take my side, choosing to put a mark against my record, rather than pay the cost of fighting for me.

Something shook me inside. I had been miraculously saved again, and I was grateful, but I experienced no joy. I felt only the shock of the accident and the attack of the other driver. But mostly, I felt anxious about the injustice. I had no voice concerning my insurance. I felt shame simply from being involved in an accident—and something deeper still.

I knew Jesus would use this circumstance for my good—if I let Him. I knew enough to sit down and practice listening to Him, using my emotions as sight, to find out what was going on.

From that accident, I learned how to listen to God in a deeper, more intentional way, and I've never been the same since. God did not cause those accidents to teach me some life-changing truths. He has nothing to do with chaos and evil. He is pure Goodness, and—if I let Him—He will use every hit from the enemy for my good.

This accident stirred up past trauma and became a defining point—an alignment in the Spirit—as Jesus took me to the root of the attacks on my life. It also led me to a prayer ministry these last 17 years called "Listening Prayer."

We are always in training. Rather than remaining

weak and vulnerable, we are being equipped to overcome—to no longer live like victims. We are taking our rightful place beside Jesus, armed with love and truth, taking ever-increasing ground for the Kingdom of God.

Blessing of an Unshakable Kingdom

Hebrews 12:25-29

I bless your spirit, in the name of Jesus Christ,
    as you stand on solid ground.
Jesus is the living Word who speaks from Heaven.
Receive His warnings
    and don't turn your back on Him.
He shakes the systems of the world,
    and the unseen powers of darkness.

I bless you with pure worship
    in His consuming light—
    thankful and overflowing
    with reverence and awe.
I bless you with security
    found in His mighty hands—
    surrounded, enveloped in His power.
Receive your heritage—your rights
    to an unshakeable Kingdom!

Blessing of Protection
Ephesians 6:10-18

In the late 1990s, Garris and I knew God was preparing us for a transition. Though we had no idea what that would look like, we did know that transitions are strategic and vulnerable to attack. An attack did come—motivated by ambition. At a weekend gathering of leaders, secret plans were going into effect that we were just learning about.

During a break in the meetings, while Garris went on a walk, I got away to a quiet place in order to be still. Jesus had my full attention, and I started praying in the Spirit. A clear scene unfolded in my mind. I saw Garris clothed in a fluid body suit, designed from some mysterious fabric, in hues of mostly golden colors, with flashes of ruby reds, deep blues—it's hard to describe. It was as close and flexible as his skin. Every step he took was accelerated as though from another dimension. I immediately knew I was seeing Garris protected by a heavenly, armored suit.

I was reminded of a scene from the film, The Matrix, where Neo is beginning to truly understand that he is operating from a different realm. He had just come under enemy fire. As he tries to dodge the bullets, he discovers that his movements are somehow accelerated, and the bullets move past him in slow motion without touching him. With the truth of his new reality dawning on his face, Neo dodges more bullets, surviving the attack with only superficial wounds. Later, he is under enemy fire—three against one. He stands his ground and puts out his hand—stopping bullets in mid-air. He defeats his powerful enemies in that skirmish.

I love those scenes.

I recognized the parallel; I was seeing Garris wearing a suit of armor from a higher reality than Earth. He was fully protected. Even as the bullets came toward him, he would take one fluid, accelerated step and not take a hit. Then I saw that there was even a force field around Garris, so that the worst of the onslaught was not even getting through.

It was the modern day version of Ephesian 6:10-18, and our authority in spiritual warfare. In that passage, Paul describes the most state-of-the-art suit of armor that would have been worn in his day. When you read that passage, imagine the best armor of our era—and then imagine it in its supernatural strength.

That armor is a picture of being clothed in God's righteousness. Our armor is Jesus.

I bless your spirit, in the name of Jesus Christ,
    with heavenly armor of warfare.
You are in a battle of life and death
    against the devil and his demons.
You cannot handle this fight on your own.
God is powerful and fully able
    to safeguard you.
Take all the help you can get:
    He wants you strong,
    He wants you prepared,
    He wants you trained
    with every needed weapon.

I bless you throughout your lifetime—
    persevering with boldness,
    wielding heaven's armament of:
    right-standing—clothed in righteousness,
    moving at accelerated peace,
    shielded in a force field of faith,
    fearless in deliverance,
    mighty in the Word of the Lord,
    alert and battle-strong in prayer,
    freedom-fighters of truth.

I bless you with a love for God
    and a love for His Word—
    an indispensable weapon.
Be blessed as you commune with God,
    praying always in the Spirit.

I bless you with grace.
I bless you with pure grace.
I bless you with nothing but grace.

Blessing of Rest
Hebrews 4:6-16; I John 3:20

Hebrews 4:12 became a life verse for me around 1982, while on a pastor's retreat. Our friends, Stan and Ginger Simmons, were the regional overseers for the state of Montana where Garris and I pioneered our first church. We were new and young, and these retreats were lifesavers. The encouragement we were given and the love and care we were shown was wonderful. Over a couple of days, we played together, ate together, and prayed together.

On this particular retreat, I gave a public prophetic word—a rare thing for me at that time in my life. We had all been praying over each other in the meeting, one couple at a time. God clearly gave me a Scripture I had read but never studied or been taught. I could only remember that it was something about God's word being so sharp and powerful that He was able to discern the very motive and intent of our hearts and teach us what was of the Spirit and what was not. I thought this Scripture was for the couple we were praying for, but I distinctly heard, "No, it's for them"—referring to another couple, whose turn to receive prayer would come later.

I forgot about the word until early the following morning, when Holy Spirit reminded me. I searched out the passage and was struck by a sense of wonder at God's heart and protection. His words were that powerful—able to bring discernment and deliver us to safety.

When it came time that day to pray over the couple God had highlighted to me, my prophetic word went something like, "Hebrews 4 says that God's word is sharp and powerful and living. He is always ready to show you the right way to go—what is of His Spirit and what is not. He will give you discernment, show you what is right and what is wrong and help you to make wise decisions. This discernment and wisdom is a great gift."

It was simple and short. The meeting ended and most of the women decided to go swimming. We congregated on the far side of the pool, hanging out together and talking. It was a stunning day and we were all soaking in the sunshine and friendship.

We became aware of a commotion at the entrance to the pool area. It was the couple I had given the word to, having what looked like a heated argument. The husband pulled away, walked all round the far side of the pool, marched right up to us, and stopped in front of me. Verbally punishing me in public, he angrily and loudly said, "I don't receive the word you spoke. It was not from God. You were totally wrong, and my wife and I don't appreciate what you said to us. We are packed and leaving early for home." With that, he turned around and marched off.

In complete silence, we all watched until they disappeared. I was speechless, and as the silence lengthened and thickened, I didn't trust my emotions any longer to hear what might be said by any of the women. I got up, stepped into the pool, dipped under the surface, and started swimming, only coming up for air. I swam for a long while. It was the perfect place to cry.

Hebrews 4:12-13 is a picture of literally wrestling with God, by letting His words pierce my heart to awaken belief—belief that I am called to stop living from all my

185

self-effort and works and rest in the complete, finished work of the Cross of Jesus Christ. That day, I processed what had taken place, letting Jesus cut through and divide between what was Spirit and truth, what was a lie from the enemy, and what was my hurt, defensive, self-protected heart.

We are often in a struggle of some kind. Why not struggle well? Allow His living, powerful words to "pin you down" with His promise to set you free—free from your ungodly beliefs about God, yourself, and life.

I bless your spirit, in the name of Jesus Christ,
    with rest from all your self-effort,
    self-condemnation, self-hatred,
    and self-defensiveness.

Hear what Holy Spirit is saying.
You are no longer pinned down by the enemy
    under the grief of injustice.
You are no longer under the hold of punishment;
    trapped in family history,
    victimized,
    living in shame,
    imprisoned by opinions and prejudices,
    held down by condemnation.

God knows all things:
    He knows your fear,
    He knows your frailty,
    He knows your wound,
    He knows you, more than you know yourself,
    He is greater than sum of your broken parts.

I bless you with comfort as you glimpse
    the Father's heart:
    His compassion for the broken,
    His determination to reach the lost,
    His ability to save by any means necessary.
I bless you with receiving
    that same compassion for yourself.

Step into God's promise.
Say *yes* to God's rest—
    available since creation
    and continuing for all eternity.
God is at rest and He has called you to His rest;
    He is your Sabbath Rest.
At the end of your journey,
    you will know full rest and peace in God.

I bless you with a holy fear—
    a wake up call.
Don't harden your heart
    through indifference, neglect,
    or the sin of unbelief.
In the name of Jesus Christ,
    be forgiven for your unbelief—
    for not entering His rest.

Pay attention to God's voice:
    welcome discernment,
    be diligent to enter His rest,
    don't give up and drop out,
    keep at it and arrive at rest!

It's true—your effort and your work
    are to rest in the finished work of Jesus.
Instead of working to rest,
    rest to work.
I bless you with rest.

I bless you with belief:
    believe He has fully forgiven you,
    believe He loves you,
    believe He will train you in love.

Is what He paid on the Cross enough?
He paid the price
    of your independence from Him,
    and your rebellion against Him.
Will you believe Him?

Rest in what God has done for you—
    no longer striving to save yourself
    or to change yourself by your own efforts.
I bless you with dependence on God.

When God speaks, He means what He says.
His words are powerful, living, sharp,
    cutting through all your doubt and defense,
    cutting through your thoughts and intentions,
    cutting through your motives and beliefs.

You are blessed when you entrust yourself to God—
    agreeing with Him, obeying Him,
    declaring His promises,

and decreeing His word.

You have struggled well—
    you have wrestled with God
    and He won.
Instead of being pinned down by your enemy,
    you are pinned by promise—
    you are pinned to Goodness.

With an opened, humbled heart,
    you are able to hear Him,
    believe Him, obey Him, accept His help,
    walk right up to Him,
    and receive what He is ready to give.
I bless you with prospering in His rest.

Blessing of God's Approval
Galatians 1:10; John 5:44

I bless your spirit, in the name of Jesus Christ,
    with seeking Him
    and seeking His honor,
    rather than seeking honor from one another
    or living for the praises of others.

To seek approval from others
    is to be corrupted by delusions,
    tainted by self-promotion,
    motivated by human sources,
    and prevented from true spiritual authority.

I bless you with a desire to honor God—
May He be your audience of One.
Seek the glory that comes from Him—
    ask to see His glory!
It brings Him great pleasure.

When you believe Him—
    your faith is strengthened
    and your message is undiluted.
I bless you with experiencing
    the honor and favor of God.

Blessing of Might

Jeremiah 33:1-2

Be blessed, in the name of Jesus Christ,
with great and mighty things,
formed and established by the Lord!

Be blessed as you call out to the Lord—as you:
speak His truth,
proclaim His promises,
pronounce His favor,
preach in His power,
publish His stories,
read His Word,
mention His name,
make Him famous.

You will be blessed with the More:
the exceedingly great—
beyond what you can imagine.
He will give you might in wisdom
and knowledge.

Those things that were withheld—
inaccessible,
too high and out of reach,
too fortified,
isolated and hidden—
are now yours.

Lift your voice in worship to the eternal Lord.

He will show you great and mighty things
    you did not know, could not know—
    but which are now yours.

Blessing of Deliverance
Mark 9:16-23

What is often translated in English as "deliver" comes from the Greek word "sozo," which means, "to save, heal, and deliver."

In the name of the Lord Jesus Christ,
    I bless your spirit with belief that
    God is your deliverer.

It is not a question
    of whether Jesus desires to deliver you,
    or is able to deliver you.
Jesus always desires to save, heal, and deliver.

As you cry out to Jesus for help,
    now is a turnaround time:
    time to corner your doubts,
    time to face your false beliefs,
    time to ask your questions,
    time to ask God for big things,
    time to stand believing—waiting—believing.

May you experience a new day:
    new opportunities,
    new permission slips,
    new possibilities.

I bless you with ears to hear Jesus say:
    Everything is possible if you believe.

Blessing of the Holy Spirit
John 20:21-22; Acts 2:2-4, 4:29-33

I bless your spirit with acknowledging
　the Lordship of Jesus Christ,
　the Son of God.

May you receive His gift:
　His death and shed blood for your sin—
　overcoming death and hell,
　His resurrection,
　His deliverance and salvation.

In the same way Jesus breathed
　upon the disciples,
　I bless you with redemption:
　receive the Holy Spirit,
　receive His gift of eternal salvation,
　receive fullness of life,
　and be reborn from above, transformed—
　a new creation.

In the same way Holy Spirit moved
　like a mighty wind and fire upon the disciples,
　receive power from on high,
　receive the breath of the Holy Spirit,
　receive the fire of God,
　receive boldness,
　receive His commission,
　receive His anointing for great exploits.

When you are saved and baptized in the Holy Spirit,
    there is more—always more:
    be activated and anointed
    in the fruit and gifts of the Spirit—
    be rekindled with fire,
    be empowered with dominion over darkness.

And continue to be filled—
    comforted, taught, and led,
    awakened, enlivened, and reformed
    by the Holy Spirit.

Blessing of Calling
I Samuel 16:18

David was a worshiper long before he was king. He was skilled as a musician, courageous, and prudent in his speech. And it was seen that God was with him.

I bless your spirit, in the name of Jesus Christ,
    with a heart of worship,
    your love for Jesus ignited—
    deepening and enlarging your capacity for more.

I bless you with right relationships
    in the community you are called to serve:
    honoring God by honoring others,
    stewarding well all God gives you,
    faithful with what you have inherited,
    with generosity in your giving.

You are in training—
    ready to risk for the Kingdom,
    ready to lay down your life for the King.
I bless you with valor in all your battles—
    combat-ready, standing with Jesus—together.

I bless you with the Word of the Lord
    as your mighty weapon—
    your speech filled with discernment
    and divine Wisdom.

I bless you with increased skill in your talents,

an activation of the prophetic in your calling,
and anointing to minister healing.

May it be seen and spoken of you—
The Lord is with you.

Blessing of Supernatural Favor I
I Chronicles 4:9

When I first read Bruce Wilkinson's book, The Prayer of Jabez, *I outlined it on a slip of paper. I kept that outline in my Bible and have prayed I Chronicles 4:9 off and on ever since. I've turned this prayer into a blessing. God's presence is our greatest wealth — our highest value.*

I bless your spirit, in the name of Jesus Christ,
    with an impartation of supernatural favor.
May your ultimate act of worship
    be a declaration of God's unlimited goodness.
God is Truth and He is Goodness.
Your greatest wealth is His constant presence
    and His blessing upon you.

Declare the Lordship of Jesus,
    making this your prayer:

> *Abba Father,*
> *Let it be with me just as you have spoken.*
> *I yield entirely to your will,*
> *to your power, to your purposes.*
> *Nothing is impossible with you.*
> *My highest value is your presence —*
> *show me your glory.*

May the Lord be your utmost ambition.
I bless you with increase:
    more influence,

more expansion,
more opportunities—
not to build your kingdom
but for God's Kingdom.

May you yield your strengths to His authority.
Couple your weakness to His supernatural power.
Experience God doing what only He can do.

Be blessed by the knowledge
    that His hand is with you
    and upon you.
Under the weight of His glory
    you are covered by the blood of Jesus,
    you are filled with His provision and plenty,
    you are anointed with His favor,
    you are overcome with His manifest presence—
    blessed beyond reason.

May you yield your right to yourself—
    now dead to self and alive in Christ Jesus,
    no longer independent or self-determined,
    led only by Him.

I bless you with strategies to choose Him—
    to be sustained by Him,
    to be empowered by Him,
    to live under His fountain of blessings.

I bless you with fullness—
    thirsting and hungering for more.

Only the touch of His hand—
　　only His glory and favor,
　　His power and boldness,
　　His enthusiasm—
　　turns this world around.

I bless you with deliverance from evil:
　　from chaos without inner peace,
　　from trouble without solutions,
　　from confusion without hope,
　　from punishment without resolution,
　　from sorrow without comfort,
　　from fear without healing love.

Identify any lurking evil—command it
　　to submit under the hand of God.
Step into the spotlight of God's manifest presence:
　　where there is nothing hidden,
　　where all is in the light,
　　where all shams are exposed,
　　where all fraud is seen for what it is,
　　where light overcomes darkness.

I bless you with deliverance
　　so that you will not cause pain:
　　the pain of grieving Holy Spirit,
　　harming your loved ones,
　　or hurting yourself.

In the name of Jesus Christ,
　　be delivered from evil,
　　be delivered from the hurt of evil,

be delivered from perpetrating evil
be delivered from the evil one.

Where there has been death,
I speak life to your spirit, soul, and body—
I bless you with life!

Blessing of Supernatural Favor II
Isaiah 60

I bless your spirit, in the name of Jesus Christ,
    with the bright glory of the Lord
    appearing over you.
Even as the whole earth is wrapped in darkness—
    the people sunk deep in its depths—
    God is shining brighter on you.

Shine into the darkness:
    nations will come to your light,
    leaders of nations will come
    to the brightness of His dawn over you.

Look in amazement—look around you:
    He is drawing people to you,
    He is reuniting family,
    He is sending heavenly angelic help.

I bless you with God's favor attending your cause:
    your message being heard,
    your heart bursting with overflow,
    your face radiating more glory.

May you reap great joy,
    with restored hope and a healed heart,
    for all that you have sown in past seasons:
    all the gracious giving,
    all the love,
    all the prayers,

all the tears in intercession,
all the blessings,
all coming back to you.

I bless you with supernatural favor:
    your children returning from far away places
    and a stream of abundance—
    all that you need and more—flowing to you.

You are backed by the name of your God,
    the Holy One of Israel.
You are showered with His splendor.

Welcome these gifts as a blessing
    to *be* a blessing.
These doors of favor are open continually—
    day and night.

From your heart of worship,
    be bathed in God's glory.
Where you were once afflicted and despised,
    you are now an everlasting pride—
    a joy from generation to generation.

God is your Savior, your Redeemer,
    your Champion.
Hear His words to you:

    I will administrate with peace.
    I will oversee with justice.
    I will surround you with safety.

I will be your eternal glory and light —
your days of grief are over.
The least of you will become a thousand —
mighty in strength.
I planted you — you are the work of my own hands.
I will display my glory through you.
I, the Lord, will act swiftly —
I will make heaven's destiny happen
at the right time.

Blessing of Wealth
Luke 16:1-13

bless you, in the name of Jesus Christ,
  in your assignment and calling.
May you wisely use possessions
  and resources as God intended—
  making the most of your opportunities.

May you be smart, shrewd,
  and wise for what is right.
Use every adversity to stimulate creative living:
  fix your eyes on the essentials,
  be content without complacency,
  contend—don't just get by on good behavior.

May you discern the times
  with a Throne Room perspective.
Be cunning—not only concerning
  the work of the enemy,
  but also concerning the Kingdom of God.

All that you have belongs to God,
  and you are His steward.
Be prudent with the use of your possessions,
  which are to be used for the benefit of others.
You don't earn your way to Heaven,
  but your attitude toward ownership
  reflects either your submission to the lordship
  of Jesus Christ, or your rebellion against Him.

How you use your material possessions
    is a legitimate sign of your fitness
    to receive true riches of Heaven—
    a reflection of your relationship with God.

I bless you with fulfilling your mandate.
Be honest in the small things,
    and you will be honest in the big things.
Be faithful and generous
    in the use of this world's wealth,
    so that you can be entrusted with true riches.
Be faithful in your stewardship
    of what belongs to others,
    and you will be given your own.
Be on the alert! Be shrewd for what is right!

I bless you with eternal riches.

Blessing of the Breath of God

Ezekiel 37:1-14; Roman 4:17; Job 33:4

*God's breath is His creative, spoken word. He spoke Adam
into being (Genesis 2:7). He breathed into him the breath
of life. In the same way, God will breathe life back into His
people. The dry bones in Ezekiel represent the condition of
hopelessness and the miracle required to restore promise.
God breathes resurrection life to those who are spiritually
dead—He will breathe life back into His Church.*

In the name of Jesus Christ,
   I bless your spirit with life and living.
To any part of you that is lifeless,
   a miracle is required to bring you back to life.

Do you doubt that these very dry bones can live?
I prophesy to those dead bones:

In the name of Jesus Christ,
   who gives life to the dead,
   who calls those things which do not exist
   as though they did,
   I declare God's desire for you,
   for your redemption,
   for your deliverance,
   for your transformation.

I prophesy over what has died or is dying:
   a nation that needs to be brought back to God,
   a home that has been ravaged

and needs healing—
listen to the word of God—
receive the breath of God and live.

I prophesy to your very dry soul,
to your exiled heart—
despondent and hopeless—
listen to the word of God,
receive the breath of God and live.

God will cause breath to enter you,
and you will come alive.
and you will know that He is God.

By the breath of the omnipresent God,
I call to the winds
from the four quarters of the earth:
Come breath of God—
come with your creative power,
blow life into every void and barren place.
I bless you with alignment to your inheritance—
to promise, provision and favor.

I bless you with Holy Spirit wind
hovering over you:
creating, resuscitating, reviving, restoring,
and filling you with hope and a future.

Receive His breath of passion—
unearth and discard what holds you down:
come out of your religious systems.
come out of your barrenness.

come out of your captivity.
come out and live!

Hear the Word of the Lord:

> *I will dig up your graves*
> *and bring you out alive.*
> *You will know that I am God.*
> *I will breathe life into you*
> *and you will live.*

Come and join the army of the living:
receive Resurrection Life,
receive His breath of life on dead relationships,
receive His breath of life on dead inheritances,
receive His breath of life on dead dreams.

When God decrees a word,
He has spoken it,
He has done it,
and He will bring it to pass.
By His word, He made you,
and He breathes life into you.

ACKNOWLEDGMENTS

Our friends, Bobbi and Mike Allstott: You bless our family in so many ways. Because of your generosity and gift of *The Passion Translation*, my heart was especially captured in a new way by the love of Jesus, the Shepherd King, through the Song of Songs. Thank you for your love!

Our children, Anna and David: You are great treasures of infinite value. I can't express how much I love you. Your dad and I impart blessings over you every day, declaring your destiny and heritage. Thank you for being the ones we practice on the most—both in learning the depth and width of love. May these blessings open doors to your callings and your unique destinies.

Our daughter, Anna: I would not be putting writing into print if you weren't part of this process. You make writing possible in so many ways. Thank you for all your help and expertise, encouragement and patience. Thank you for the times you even did extra household jobs when I was holed up, lost in writing, and unmindful of "things to be done."

My husband, Garris: I trust you—I trust your heart—I trust you more than any other human being. You are always my strongest, most ardent supporter in anything and everything. You are my best friend. You even feed me breakfast every day—starting in the dark, wee hours of the morning, as we both search out what God is downloading to us—and then transcribing it. I love you, husband of mine.

I would also like to thank those who made possible the following Bible translations, which I used when crafting the blessings:

The Message
New American Standard Bible
The Passion Translation
Spirit-Filled Life Bible